FAIRY TALES FOR THE PSYCHE

Verena Kast

FAIRY TALES
FOR THE
PSYCHE

"Ali Baba and the Forty Thieves"
and
The Myth of Sisyphus

Translated by Vanessa Agnew

CONTINUUM • NEW YORK

1996

The Continuum Publishing Company
370 Lexington Avenue
New York, NY 10017

Ali Baba und die vierzig Räuber and *Sisyphos*
from the special edition *Glückskinder:*
Wie man das Schicksal überlisten kann
Copyright © Kreuz Verlag AG Zürich 1993
English translation Copyright © 1996
by The Continuum Publishing Company

Printed in the United States of America

Library of Congress Cataloging-in-Publication Data

Kast, Verena, 1943–
    [Glückskinder. English. Selections]
    Fairy tales for the psyche : Ali Baba and the forty thieves and
the myth of Sisyphus / Verena Kast ; translated by Vanessa Agnew.
        p.   cm.
    Includes bibliographical references.
    ISBN 0–8264–0847–8 (hardcover : alk. paper)
    1. Mythology—Psychological aspects. 2. Psychoanalysis and
folklore. 3. Fairy tales—Psychological aspects. 4. Sisyphus
(Greek mythology)—Psychological aspects. 5. Symbolism in fairy
tales. I. Kast, Verena, 1943– Ali Baba und die 40 Räuber.
English. II. Kast, Verena, 1943– Sisyphos. English. III. Title.
BF 175.5.M95K37   1996
398'.352—dc20   95-37022
                                                            CIP

Contents

Sisyphus:
The Old Stone —The New Way

Preface

This book contains interpretations of the fairy tale "Ali Baba and the Forty Thieves" and the myth of Sisyphus. I am happy that these two different studies, which previously appeared individually, are now being published together in a special edition.

Have I truly written about fairy tales for the psyche here? Indeed I have, since the underlying theme of both works is really how human happiness can be examined through fairy tale and myth; this ultimately amounts to discovering how to wrest success from the difficulties of life. Life is hard enough for the two heroes, but even more so for the heroines. However, they do not allow themselves to be paralyzed by their problems; they see them as challenges. They are fascinated by the possibility of success, not by possible failure. All of them are fully engaged in their own lives and in the end consider their respective fates to be reasonable but alterable. This attitude of engagement, the hope for potential amelioration, and the trust that they will find creative solutions all permit them to surmount the difficulties. They do so by carefully scrutinizing what is problematic within themselves, by accepting and overcoming these problems. These characters do not seek out the one "great happiness," but rather the experience of happiness in everyday life—something that lights up when one does what needs to be done. In so doing, they emphasize devotion to life and its tasks and the experience of *being* far less than the experience of *having*. When we live like this, then life is animated: we feel connected to a pulsating life force. Following these stories in our fantasies and reflections, we too can be encouraged by the heroes and heroines to seek out our own happiness.

VERENA KAST

ALI BABA
AND THE
FORTY THIEVES

How to Really Get Rich

Open Sesame!

Even if the fairy tale, "Ali Baba and the Forty Thieves," with all its cruel particulars, were to disappear from our memory trove, the magic formula "Open sesame" that is used so imploringly in the story would still be germane, enriched as it is with fantasies from everyday life.

"Open sesame!" If you know the right formula, how to conjure up something, then even a rock can be opened—a rock that at first appears closed and impenetrable, that you would never expect to open. Embodied in this magic formula is the whole fascination that we associate with the opening of something that is closed, of locked things that have no key and are not easily cracked apart. The formula also encapsulates an initial expectation: despite the fact that we know better, we hope that something which cannot actually happen will happen.

When we are in a hopeful state of mind, fairy tales draw us in over and over again, particularly this one. There are changes in life that we really cannot fathom—and such things actually do happen. So we hope for the unexpected.

It's not just the fascination with the understanding or "opening" of something that was hitherto impermeable that entices us in this fairy tale image. It also has something to do with the fact that the opening reveals a cave full of hidden treasure, albeit not right away and not without difficulty. Nevertheless, the first image is that of a cave full of treasure laid open. The experience of opening up is linked with the vision of great brilliance, great beauty, great wealth.

The formula "Open sesame!" always occurs to us in situations of impoverishment, when we are in some way restricted—in the widest sense of the word. We think "Open sesame!" in situations when we wish more than anything that something closed would open up. We wish that we could uncover the secret, that a vision would open up before us of something that we don't have—and naturally, we hope for a new abundance, whether of a material or an ideal nature, for new sense experiences or for love, for joy in the beauty of existence, or for the new energy which life promises us.

In this context we do not speak of opening something. It is not a conscious action. Instead, something opens itself to us, something presents itself, something reveals itself. All these expressions and the associated images point to the fact that something happens externally that redirects our gaze at what is new. A view that has until now been obscured is no longer obscured. We don't do it—it happens of its own accord. But in order for it to happen we need a magic formula—which in this instance could not be simpler: "Open sesame! Sesame, open your door!"

And yet, it is not quite so simple as all that. The rock, the cave have to be perceptible in some way or another. They have to actually seek us out, or at least we have to be in the right place at the right time. We also have to take some action.

This fairy tale shows us the kinds of problems that can be associated with such a treasure trove and also how much has to be accomplished in order to get the treasure trove to relinquish its treasures.

The Story of Ali Baba
and the Forty Thieves

Once upon a time in the land of Churaran in Persia there lived
two brothers. The older brother, Kasim, was rich and cruel. The
younger, Ali Baba, had taken a poor young woman as his wife and
moreover, since he did not know how to economize, what little he had
possessed soon became even less. Finally all his worldly possessions consisted of only a roof over their heads, a donkey, and a slave named Mardschana, a young woman with a pleasing appearance and a good head on
her shoulders.

What was Ali Baba to do? After long consideration he finally decided to sell Mardschana as well. But she said to him, "Master, please don't
sell me. What little money you will get for me will soon have run through
your fingers and then you'll be in an even worse predicament than you
are now. You should take the donkey into the mountains instead and col-
lect firewood there. You will be able to sell it at market."

Ali Baba liked this idea. The very next morning he took his ax and
wended his way into the mountains with his donkey. He worked there the
whole day, then loaded the wood onto the donkey which carried it to the
town bazaar. That evening a few gold pieces jingled in Ali Baba's purse.

From that day on Ali Baba earned a meager livelihood collecting firewood and had no more worries. One day when he was busy cutting wood, there suddenly appeared in the distance a cloud of dust that approached rapidly. Soon he could make out a band of riders, wild and dangerous-looking fellows with sabers and daggers that filled him with terror. Ali Baba quickly drove his donkey into the undergrowth and climbed the nearest tree, whose thick crown hid him from the wild bunch—forty men in all.

And it was under just this tree that the riders stopped, jumped off their horses, threw their saddlebags over their shoulders and walked toward a nearby rocky outcrop that was covered in thick brush.

Then another man—judging by his clothing and his behavior he must have been their leader—appeared and called out, "Open sesame!" At exactly the same moment a door in the rocks opened, admitted the riders, and then closed behind them again.

After a while the men emerged from the rocks again and Ali Baba had the opportunity to take a closer look at them. By their wild appearance, their bearded faces, and their dark, ominous looks, he concluded that it must be none other than the terrible robber band that had long been terrorizing the area. So this was where they had the cave for hiding their loot!

The robbers fastened their now empty bags onto their saddles, mounted their horses, and disappeared as quickly as they had come. Ali Baba let out a sigh of relief. But instead of beating a quick retreat he wanted to find out whether the rock would also obey his command.

"Open sesame!" he called just as he had heard the leader of the robber band do. And lo and behold, the door opened silently and he stepped inside. Once he had entered the cave, his eyes nearly popped out of his head at the sight of all the treasure that the robbers had amassed: whole mountains of gold pieces, precious stones as big as a fist, fabric from India and China, pearls like the sands of the sea . . . Ali Baba paced the entire cave, his eyes getting wider and wider. Such treasures he would never have dared to dream of! But fear of the robbers soon shook him out of his reverie. They might be back any minute, and if they found him here that would be the end of him.

Quickly he took as many bags of gold as he could carry and gave the command, "Open sesame!" Outside he loaded the bags of gold onto the donkey and arranged a covering of firewood over the top so that no one would discover his priceless load. Then he raced home, hoping that the robbers would not notice anything and that they would not follow him.

Once safely at home, he barred the door so as to be sure that no one would come in unexpectedly. Then to his wife's complete amazement, he shook the gold onto the floor so that it jangled. His wife was beside herself with happiness, but she was also afraid. Only when Ali Baba assured her that he had taken just the smallest fraction of the robbers' horde, so that they were unlikely to notice anything, did her fears subside. Then she got to the business of counting the dinars.

"At this rate you won't be done by this evening," said Ali Baba. "And we still have to hide the money. I think the best thing to do would be to bury it in the garden." But because his wife absolutely had to know just how rich they were, she quickly ran over to the wife of the wealthy Kasim in order to borrow a bushel scale. "What sort of grain are those paupers ever going to weigh?" wondered Kasim's wife to herself when her sister-in-law made her request. And out of sheer curiosity she secretly poured some wax into the bottom of the scale before she lent it out.

While Ali Baba dug a pit in the garden, his wife measured out ten bushels of gold dinars; then together they buried the gold in the garden.

The very same day Kasim's wife got her scale back. She turned it over and lo! Stuck in the wax was a gold piece.

"So that's it!" she shrieked and ran straight to her husband. "Your brother has been pleading poverty when in reality he weighs his gold with a bushel scale."

Kasim, who had always been possessed by stinginess, greed and envy, could not sleep a wink that night. He tossed and turned. He knew that he would never sleep peacefully again if he did not find out where his brother had gotten the money.

So directly after the morning prayers he went and knocked on Ali Baba's door. Ali Baba welcomed his older brother in a friendly and fitting way, but Kasim got straight to the point and called him a hypocrite and a liar who had just been feigning poverty. "I know that you have to weigh the gold with a bushel scale when you want to know how much you have. Here is the proof!" And he waved in front of his face a dinar that his wife had picked out of the wax on the scale. "Either you tell me where you got the money or I'm going to inform the judge about you."

"I'd be happy to tell you everything, brother," said Ali Baba, who didn't know any other way out of the situation. And he reported truthfully what had happened to him the previous day. In fact, at Kasim's insistence, he even described the exact route to the robber's den. "But I don't advise you to challenge fate and go there," he warned. "Better that I share everything with you, than that I knowingly expose you to danger and that you fall into the terrible hands of the robbers." But Kasim just laughed at him. "You idiot, do you honestly think that I would pass up the opportunity to become a hundred times richer?"

With these words he ran off with all haste to town where he bought all the donkeys he could lay his hands on, so that pretty soon people started to think that he wanted to do the donkey drivers out of a job. And out of pure excitement, he could not sleep a wink this night. As soon as dawn came, he took his caravan into the mountains and soon found the rocky outcrop that Ali Baba had described to him.

"Open sesame!" he called, and the door actually opened and let him inside. When he looked around the cave and saw how much was lying about he was glad he had bought so many donkeys, since not even these would be able to carry it away all at once. But what to take first? As though possessed, he laid sacks full of gold and precious stones ready at the entrance; he carried great chests, lamps, and priceless fabrics. In his greed and obsession he completely forgot the world around him; he just grasped and clutched at things. Finally, he thought that he had enough for one day and that it was time to carry everything outside and load up the animals.

But alas! Thinking the whole time only of his riches, he had forgotten the name of the rock door. All he could recall was that it was some grain or other and he tried each of them in turn as they occurred to him: "Oats, open up!" Then, "Open barley!" Open up, wheat!"

He named one type of grain after the other. Only one could he not recall—sesame.

The rock stayed shut, and in desperation Kasim started to cry out for help. Too late, he bemoaned, to listen to his brother's advice.

Even greater was his terror when he heard hoof-beats outside. The robbers had returned. They discovered the donkeys outside the cave and of course they immediately realized what was going on.

"Open sesame!" commanded the leader of the robbers fiercely. The rock door opened and Kasim stormed out of the cave, seeking safety in flight. But he did not make it two steps when the robbers felled him with their knives. Then they dragged the body into the cave, leaving it right by the entrance as a warning to anyone who might venture to try the same thing.

Having done this, they drove the donkeys away, carried the treasure back to its place and added their latest bounty. Moments later the only evidence that the robber band had ever been there was a dust cloud receding in the distance. The surroundings were as abandoned and devoid of life as before.

Ali Baba waited two days for his brother's return, but the longer he waited the greater was his fear that the robbers had surprised Kasim in the cave. When he still had not returned on the third day, Ali Baba's terrible suspicion became almost a certainty. Finally he could stand it no longer and set off for the robbers' den. He approached very cautiously, avoiding every crackling branch. But the stillness around finally gave him a sense of security.

"Open sesame!" He called out the magic password. Oh! what horror! Right in the entrance to the cave lay the bloody corpse of his brother, proof that the robbers were not to be toyed with.

Ali Baba loaded the dead Kasim onto his donkey so that at least he could be given a decent burial and took a round-about route home. He didn't want to run into anyone.

At home he was still afraid that the robbers, having discovered the disappearance of the body, would follow his tracks and exact their terrible revenge.

In his distress, he confided in his clever slave, Mardschana. "Master, that's really horrible," said the young woman. "Don't tell anyone, don't breathe a single word. It would be best to let it be known that Kasim has died of a dreadful illness. And in order to be sure, make your sister-in-law your second wife. Then we'll all move into your brother's house."

Ali Baba followed Mardschana's advice word-for-word. He settled in the city, took over his brother's business and in one stroke he was a wealthy man.

Nor indeed did the robbers stay inactive. That the body had disappeared proved that there was someone else who knew both their hiding-place as well as the secret password. They spread out through the whole area in an effort to find the intruder. The bravest of them took on the most difficult assignment: to comb the city that lay in closest proximity to the cave. The leader of the robber band advised him to disguise himself as a merchant so as not to draw any attention to himself if he were to question people surreptitiously . This robber proved to be particularly sly and in no time learned who had died recently and who had unexpectedly become rich as a result. More than that he did not need to know.

Finding himself in front of Ali Baba's house, he tried to commit it to memory. But he found that all the houses in the city resembled one another as one egg does another. So he secretly drew a cross on the door thinking that he would be able to find it again at night. Then he hurried back to his leader to report how cleverly he had contrived everything.

Mardschana, however, was even shrewder than the robber. Although she suspected street urchins when she saw the cross, just to be sure she took a piece of chalk and drew similar crosses on all the houses in the street.

At twilight the robbers set off to attack Ali Baba's house. They hid their sharp sabers and knives under their merchants' clothes and thus disguised went to the city. However, they could not find the house since all the houses in the street bore the same chalk cross and so they had to return home unsuccessful in their mission. Back in the robber's den they sat in judgment over the spy who had let himself be outwitted.

"He must be judged according to our custom," said the leader of the band and the rest of them concurred. So did the robber who was being judged since he knew that he would never be able to continue to live in shame among the robbers. Since it had always been an unwritten robbers' law that whoever failed had to forfeit his life, the robber stood bravely before the leader, who cut off his head with a single blow.

Then Ahmed, the strongest of the group stepped forward. "Brave men! I alone am capable of carrying out such an assignment. And if I don't lead you to the precise spot, then may the same fate befall me." "So be it, Ahmed! If you succeed then all the booty from the house will go to you. If not, then you will lose your head!" answered the robber leader in a serious tone.

Yet things didn't go any better for Ahmed than they had for his predecessor. He did in fact find the right house, cut himself in the finger, and with a drop of blood made a sign in an inconspicuous place next to the door. But this too Mardschana discovered the next day when she was returning from the market where she had just bought some fish. This second sign proved to her that it was no pure coincidence and so she furnished all the houses in the street with the same mark. Only so as not to have to cut her own finger, she simply used the fish's blood.

Yet again the robbers came in vain to the city. Ahmed got shorter by a head and the robber leader fumed with rage. "Tomorrow I will go myself to the city. No one is going to lead me around by the nose. In the meantime, go and find twenty mules and forty big oil jars of which you are to fill only two with oil. And woe be to anyone who gets anything wrong, you bunch of fools!" he added menacingly.

The robbers crept off to their places like whipped dogs and slept fitfully until morning.

It did not occur to the robber leader to make a sign. When he stood in front of Ali Baba's house he simply counted which house it was in the street and before it was even getting dark he was back with his companions.

In the meantime they had carried out all of his orders. Nineteen mules with empty oil jars stood ready and only the twentieth animal carried two full jars.

"Now listen to me carefully!" ordered the leader in a quiet voice. "When we get to just outside the city gate each of you is to climb into a jar. You are not to move until I give you the sign!"

Night fell. In the pale light of the moon the robber leader disguised as a merchant led his caravan of mules through the streets in which Ali Baba lived. He counted the houses and knocked on the right door.

"Who is knocking so late at night?" asked a man's voice from inside and the robber leader answered, "I am a merchant and I have come from afar. I have just arrived in your city and since all the bazaars and inns are closed I would like to know if it wouldn't be possible for you to put me and my mules up for the night."

Ali Baba opened the door and saw a strange merchant with tired animals standing in the doorway.

"Greetings, brother, make yourself at home here," he said and led the guest into the inner chamber after telling a servant to take care of the animals.

What more could the robber leader wish? In his wildest dreams it would never have occurred to the unsuspecting Ali Baba that this was his bloodthirsty enemy, the less so when his guest offered him various things that he had supposedly wanted to sell in the city.

They ate, drank, and conversed until late at night when Mardschana wanted to fill the empty oil lamps. But in the whole house there was not a drop of oil to be found. Then it occurred to her that the strange merchant had just offered to sell her master oil. Surely he would not mind parting with a few liters for his friends. She took a jug and hurried down to the courtyard. The servant had unloaded the oil jars from the mules and they were now leaning against a wall. Just as Mardschana was about to undo the first jar a hollow sound emerged from inside, "Is it time yet, captain?"

Anyone else would have fainted in fright, but not Mardschana, who right away figured out what was lurking in the plump oil jar. Quick-wittedly she whispered in a disguised voice, "Not yet. Wait a moment!"

Then she went from jar to jar. At each of them she repeated the same trick until she came to the end of the row and had counted thirty-eight robbers.

Only in the last two jars did she really find oil and this gave her an idea. She carried a large cauldron from the kitchen, poured in oil from the jars and lit a fire under the cauldron. Then she fanned the fire until the oil began to boil and poured the bubbling oil into the jars directly onto the heads of the robbers. The bandits who had long held the area in fear and terror died miserable deaths.

Having thus rendered the robbers harmless, she went back into the house as though nothing had happened. She filled up the lamps, put on her dancing outfit, and accompanied by the servant Abdallah, who held a drum in his hand, re-entered the hall.

Ali Baba was impressed by her and said to his guest, "Sir, this woman is really a treasure. She is not only an outstanding servant, but also the most charming dancer I have ever seen. And besides, she is extraordinarily clever; who else would have come up with the delightful idea of increasing our pleasure with the sight of her dancing?"

The robber leader just nodded, cleverly hiding his rage and impatience. He longed for the moment when he could exact his revenge—and now he would have to wait even longer!

Abdallah beat the drum and Mardschana swayed to the dance. She moved so gently and gracefully, her feet barely touching the floor, and her youthful countenance beamed like a newly blossoming flower in the spring.

The dance came to an end. The young woman took the drum from Abdallah's hand and bowed before Ali Baba, receiving a reward from him. She got her dinar and then stepped up to the false merchant with the same act. The robber leader also tried to take a dinar out of his breast pocket but in so doing accidentally revealed the dagger that he kept concealed there.

At that moment Mardschana grabbed the dagger and stabbed the villain in the heart so that right then and there he breathed his last and exhaled his evil soul.

"You unfortunate one! What have you done?" shouted Ali Baba angrily. "You won't escape punishment!" "Calm down, my lord," responded Mardschana calmly. "This man was no foreign merchant, but the head of the terrible robber band who wanted to do you in. Come with me and see the proof for yourself!"

And she led him to the courtyard and the oil jars. To Ali Baba's horror there was no oil in the jars but instead thirty-eight dead robbers. And then she told him about how she had found the signs and twice deceived the robbers.

Ali Baba could not praise Mardschana's cleverness enough. As a token of his thankfulness he released her from slavery and married her to his son, since he had long been aware that the two young people were not indifferent to one another. And a cleverer and truer daughter-in-law he could hardly have hoped for.

However there was one thing that Mardschana could not account for: what had happened to the two missing robbers. At the time, Ali Baba had counted forty robbers apart from the leader outside the cave, but there were only thirty-eight in the oil jars. What she could not have known was that the robber leader had disposed of the two of them with his very own hands.

Thus for an entire year Ali Baba did not venture into the cave and only when he had persuaded himself that no one had been there the whole time was he able to get some peace.

Until the end of his days he lived in peace and prosperity, fetching from the robbers' den only as much as he needed. And all his life Mardschana was the only person who knew the secret, since Ali Baba had learned only too well what envy and greed could do.[1]

Stories About Death

The Framing Story

"Ali Baba and the Forty Thieves" is the story that Scheherezade told the Sultan Scheherban on the 270th night. In telling him the story, she prevented the Sultan from killing her. Hitherto he had spent every night with a different woman only to kill her the following morning.

Such brutal behavior, reminiscent of the knight Bluebeard, has of course a prehistory. This prehistory, which constitutes the framework of the stories of A *Thousand and One Nights*, is very important since "Ali Baba and the Forty Thieves" also needs to be seen in conjunction with the problem that is dealt with in the context of that framework:

In the name of God, the good and merciful, peace be with our Lord Muhammad, the highest envoy of God, and with his family and friends; peace be with them until the Day of Judgment. The destiny of the forbearers be a lesson to those who are to come. May they learn from it and diligently read the lessons of the past. Find in these stories, called the

"Thousand and One Nights," advice and wisdom, things reported here that were once talked of by the people.

A long time ago there ruled a king on the islands of India and China. He was rich and had many servants and many soldiers. His sons were called Scheherban and Schahseman. Scheherban was the elder; Schahseman ruled over Samarkand in Persia and ruled for twenty happy years. One day the older king was seized by a longing for his younger brother. He called his vizier and ordered him to travel to Schahseman and bring him back. The younger brother obeyed the summons immediately, had camels and mules armored and got underway with his stately retinue. His own vizier took over the job of governing in his absence. But it so happened that Schachseman remembered that he had left something behind in his castle; quickly he hurried back and surprised his wife in forbidden love with a slave. Boiling rage rose up in him, so he drew his sword and stabbed them both; thereupon he traveled on until he came to the capital city of his brother. He had a messenger announce his arrival and Scheherban received him with pomp and circumstance, embraced him, and greeted him joyfully. But the memory of his wife's infidelity gnawed at king Schahseman's soul so that his face grew pale and the strength in his body ebbed. None of the festivities could cheer him out of his gloominess. Scheherban thought that it was homesickness that was eating away at him. One day full of concern he asked him, "Dear brother I see that your cheeks are becoming pale and that you have some secret worry that is lodged in your soul." To which Schahseman replied, "There's a sickness torturing me inside," and he told him what had happened upon his departure. Then his brother left to go off riding by himself and Schahseman stayed behind, full of sadness and vexation. However, in the castle inhabited by Schahseman there were several windows through which he could see into his brother's garden. Looking out, he saw how twenty slaves, both men and women, emerged from the doors of the palace and in their midst walked his brother's wife, a woman of exquisite beauty and stature. They walked over to a pond where the women undressed and sat *themselves before the men. The queen called Masud, a slave, over to her, embraced and caressed him. And the other slaves did them same, whiling away the day with kisses and love. When Schahseman saw this, he said to himself, "In truth my brother is in a worse predicament than I." His cares and worries evaporated and he ate and drank once again.*

When the king Scheherban returned from the hunt and saw that his brother had regained his former strength and color and was happily eating and drinking, he said to him, "Dear brother, yesterday you were so pale and weak and today I see you in full health. Was has happened?" To which his brother responded, "You know my brother that when I set off with my retinue to come and visit you I had already left the capital, when it suddenly occurred to me that I had forgotten something in my castle; I found my wife keeping company with a slave and in my rage I killed them both. I became pale and weak because I couldn't forget what happened. But the reason I have recovered my erstwhile appearance, that is something that I cannot tell you." However, Scheherban pressed his brother for an answer and would give him no peace so that finally he told him what had transpired in the garden. The sultan shouted full of anger and wrath, "I want to see their sins with my own eyes!" Schahseman gave him the following advice, "Tell her you want to go hunting. Then come and hide with me so that you can watch them in secret."

So Scheherban let it be known that he wanted to go on a long trip and he took his retinue out of the city. Having made camp, he told his page, "Don't let anyone in here." Then he disguised himself and secretly returned to his brother. There he sat full of anticipation at the window looking out at the blossoming garden. After a while the gate opened and his wife appeared with the slaves and they carried on just as Schahseman had said until the afternoon prayers were called. When Scheherban saw this, he was speechless with pain and called, "Brother, let's leave here. I don't want to have anything more to do with governing! Let's travel around until we find someone who is in the same state we are in. If we don't come across anyone may death take us from our misery!"

They got underway, departing through a hidden door in the palace and traveled for many days and nights. One day they arrived in a peaceful place. There was the rustling of leafy trees and a sweet spring that rippled through the undergrowth by the sea. They drank from the spring and rested for a while. Suddenly a storm blew up and the sea roared and a large column rose into the sky, furrowed its way through the waves toward the land. When the two brothers saw this they were very frightened and they climbed into a tall tree.

It was however the spirit of our Lord Salomo (Peace be with him!). He was very large and had a big head and a broad chest. On his head he carried a box made of glass that was locked with four steel padlocks. The spirit sat under the tree in which the two brothers were sitting, took the box off his head and opened the locks with four keys. Out of the box he drew a wonderful young woman with a sweet mouth, beautiful breasts, and a face that resembled the full moon. "Oh beloved of my soul. You most beautiful and perfect of all women whom I seduced before anyone else could know you! Let me sleep in your lap." Lord Salomo laid his head on her knee, stretched himself out and started snoring so that soon it sounded like thunder rolling in the distance. With this, the woman raised her head and by chance glimpsed Scheherban sitting with his brother in the tree. Slowly she laid the spirit's head onto the ground and with a sign gave them to understand that she would like them to climb down to her. One of them answered however, "Excuse us madam, if we don't come down." To which she replied, "If you don't come down I will wake up the spirit, my husband, and he will eat you." Giving them a friendly wink, she enticed the brothers to climb down to her. Then she said that she would like to have her way with them. But the brothers said, "By the Almighty, don't demand that of us. We are afraid of the spirit." She said, "If you don't lie down beside me then I swear I will wake up the spirit so that he can kill you." So the brothers did as they were told. Then she took a bag out of her clothes and removed ninety-eight silver rings, saying, "Do you know what these rings mean? They come from the ninety-eight men who've submitted to me. Now give me your rings as well so that I know that it's been a hundred men with whom I've deceived the horrible, ugly spirit. He put me in this box, you see, and makes me live in the depths of the sea so that I stay virtuous and belong only to him. The monster doesn't realize that a woman's will can't be controlled by anyone!"

When the two brothers heard this they were absolutely astonished and they cried, "Only God in Heaven can protect us! We'll have to turn to him for help against the cunning of women. Because really nothing compares with this one!" But the woman said to them, "Get on your way!"

So as they walked on Scheherban said, "Listen brother, this little adventure is even stranger than ours. Here we have a spirit who stole a woman on her wedding night and locked her in a glass box. He locked her up with four padlocks and sunk her to the bottom of the raging sea so that he could snatch her away from fate. And even she has been unfaithful one hundred times. Truly, there are no faithful women! We should return comforted to our kingdoms and resolve never to marry again." So they turned around and went along until night was starting to fall; on the third day they arrived back home. They took up the throne again and all the princes and nobles in the land gathered around them. The king proclaimed that he would like to move back into the city. He retired to his castle and summoned his vizier. His vizier was to kill his wife and this he did forthwith. Thereupon, the king went to the slave women and he killed them all with his sword. Then he summoned others and swore that every night he would choose one and the following morning have her executed since there wasn't a single virtuous woman in the whole world. His brother Schahseman traveled back straight away, returning to his kingdom.

Meanwhile Sultan Scheherban commanded his vizier to bring him a slave, upon which the vizier brought him one of the prince's daughters. The king did as he had promised and ordered the vizier to chop off her head the following day. The vizier obeyed his lord's instructions and did the woman in. After that the vizier brought him another daughter of one *of the country's nobility and she too lost her head in the morning. And so it continued until finally there were no more daughters in all the land; the mothers and fathers wept and wailed, cursed the king, and called upon Heaven to send help and retribution.*

Now it so happened that the chief vizier, who had had to kill the women at the sultan's instigation, had two daughters. The older of the two was called Scheherezade and the younger, Dinarsad. Scheherezade knew many books and had an incredibly good memory. She had learned poems by heart and knew stories and speeches of kings and wise men. One day she said to her father, "Dear father, I want to confide in you. I want you to marry me to the Sultan Scheherban because I want to rid the world of his evil deeds. Otherwise I want to die like the other women have." When her father heard these words he was deeply shocked and he said, "You fool, don't you know what the king has sworn? If I take you to him he will have you killed!" Scheherezade countered by saying, "Take me to him even if he's to have me killed." When he heard this her father got angry and shouted, "Why do you so stubbornly insist on plunging straight into danger? Have you lost your mind? He who isn't prudent in his actions has only himself to blame for his own misfortune and whoever doesn't consider the implications of his actions has no friends in the world. You know how the saying goes: If you go looking for trouble you'll find it." But Scheherezade simply answered, "I won't change my mind. If you don't take me to the king, then I'll go by myself and I'll tell him that you've been denying me to the king and that you want to keep me from him."

The narrator goes on to relate how the vizier after having threatened and pleaded in vain, made up his mind and went to the sultan Scheherban, kissed the ground and said to him:

"My Lord, tomorrow night I will bring you my daughter." The sultan was incredulous and asked, "What does this mean? Haven't I sworn by the Heavens above that on the morrow I will have her killed? And if you do not obey then I will have you yourself killed." The vizier

answered, "Oh my king, I have said all this to her myself but she won't listen to me. All she wants is to spend this night with you." The sultan spoke, "Well go then, prepare her arrival and bring her to me tonight." The vizier returned home and informed his daughter about what the king had commanded, saying, "God grant that I don't yearn for you." Scheherezade was overjoyed, got her affairs in order and said to her younger sister Dinarsad, "Dear sister, listen closely to what I'm going to say. When I've spent a little while with the sultan I will send for you. When you arrive and see that the sultan is no longer occupied with me then say to me, 'Dear sister, if you aren't sleeping then won't you tell us one of your wonderful stories so we can pass the night away'. This alone can save the world and me. Only this will divert the king from his unholy undertakings." All this Dinarsad promised to do.

When night fell Scheherazade went to the sultan. He received her tenderly and joked with her but she began to cry. Scheherban asked, "Why are you crying?" she answered, "Oh king, at home I have a sister. Please let me say farewell to her tonight." So the sultan ordered someone to send for Dinarsad. She came and waited a while until the sultan and her sister had caressed and rested a little and then she let out a deep sigh and said, "If you aren't sleeping then won't you tell us one of your wonderful stories so that we can while away the night. When day breaks I'll say farewell to you since I don't know if I will see you again in the morning again."

Scheherazade asked the sultan for permission and when he granted it she was very happy and thus she began . . .²

For a thousand and one nights Scheherazade told stories and during this time she also bore the sultan three sons—apparently he was not aware of this. After she had told the last story she showed him the three boys and for the children's sake pleaded with him to spare her life, since there was no one else who could care for them as well as she.

The sultan said to her, "Oh Scheherazade, by Allah, I had already absolved you before these children came . . ."[3]

The sultan also honored the vizier by saying, "Allah protected you so that you could give me your noble daughter as a wife, the woman who is responsible for stopping me from killing the daughters of the land. I find her to be noble and pure, chaste and virtuous . . ."[4]

Scheherazade succeeded in healing the sultan by freeing him from the compulsion to kill women. These stories had healing properties—Scheherazade is probably the first to use fairy stories as a successful form of therapy. She was able to convey a new image of womanhood to the sultan, but also to impart a new way of life. Besides this, she was able to bring him closer to her so that he could only reach the boys through her. However, even without the children he would have allowed her to live and would have gone ahead and married her. This seems to me to be important since it points to the fact that he has gained a new relationship to her as a woman.

The Compulsion to Kill[5]

In the interpretation of fairy stories, we proceed with the assumption that every story expresses a typical existential problem. The course of action that the hero or heroine takes during the story—something that always involves personal development—helps him or her to overcome the problem during the course of the tale.[6]

The framing story from A Thousand and One Nights represents a comprehensive dilemma which is overcome through telling and listening to stories. Yet the individual stories can certainly be read independently, with each story referring to a different human condition that has to be overcome.[7]

At the center of the framing story is Scheherban, who swears never to marry again after he decides that there are no faithful women. Every night he spends with a different young woman, whom he then orders killed the following morning. This is his revenge—he is driven by a compulsion for revenge. His intention is simply to avenge what has happened to him. Yet the end of all life becomes a very real possibility if all the daughters in the land are to be killed. Scheherban is reminiscent not only of Bluebeard, whose handiwork is put to a stop after he has killed several women,[8] but also of the legendary dragon that every year demands a young woman to devour.

Scheherban spends a night with each of the young women, but he doesn't enter into any kind of relationship with them. He simply *takes* the women; he robs them. Considering that the women probably know that they are to be killed the following day, one can hardly conceive of it as being an intoxicating wedding night, but rather one of sadomasochistic practices and torture. The women are certainly unlikely to be allowed to experience any kind of pleasure.

Fairy stories, however, are also symbolic stories. This means that narrative characteristics that refer to real life always refer to something on an abstract level as well. Concrete everyday relationships also imply intrapsychic relationships with the different aspects of our personalities. This sort of interpretation is what is known as an interpretation at the subject level. People and situations that we encounter in the concrete outside world can also be seen as intrapsychic personality traits. Thus the sultan may have a tortuous, volatile relationship with his intrapsychic feminine side. Because women are not the way that he imagines them to be they must be eradicated. What disturbs him in particular is their cunning. Feminine characteristics— above all the fascinating feminine aspects that might integrate his psyche—are not allowed to exist and have to be destroyed. Therefore, he is also unable to enter into a close relationship with a real-life woman. Were this not the case, he could become dependent on her, and this is the very thing that he cannot allow. Doing so would result in a loss of self-worth. Instead he has to continually issue death warrants so that he is master of all women, and master of all that is feminine within himself. The feminine becomes enslaved. He controls life destructively. Nor does he give women a chance to show themselves. He denies himself the option of saying "Open sesame!" and of finding out that sesame really can open. In this instance sesame cannot open. People become as destructive as Scheherban when they feel hurt and disappointed. The depths of the disappointment correspond to the degree of revenge.

We know the reason for Scheherban's behavior: both his brother Schahseman's wife and his own wife deceived their husbands. As soon as the husbands were out of the house they slept with slaves. The women are in other words "unfaithful," and to make matters worse they are unfaithful with slaves, with men who are in a socially inferior position and are thus, perhaps, deemed exotic and dangerous. In other words, the women let in things that are usually suppressed—and seem to have a lot of fun doing so. If one interprets this story at the subject level, it would go something like this: barely has the sultan relinquished control over his psyche when he finds his feminine side getting entangled in a sexual adventure involving sides of himself that he usually enslaves and suppresses.

When characteristics of ourselves that we usually have well under control are suddenly revived, then we feel a lot of pain. The sort of overpowering emotion that arises because of a passionate love affair can result in aspects of ourselves emerging that we find undesirable. Stuff comes up that we would rather

keep in the depths of our soul—our shadow makes itself perceptible. Such experiences in which the shadow is activated can be
very vital, but in hindsight we may feel a lot of pain. Maybe we
even try to blame someone else for the fact that we have let our-
self go and we try to punish them.

Furthermore, on a purely concrete object level, the problematic relationship between the sexes is illustrated by the story
of a spirit that keeps a woman locked in a glass box at the bottom of the sea so that she stays true to him. He has stolen the
woman away before she could belong to anyone else and now
he holds her captive. And yet she deceives him in order to
make it clear to him that he cannot possess her, that this rapa-
cious way of dealing with women ultimately can lead only to
cunning and deception.

Once again this picture embodies the problem outlined in
the framing story. It was the ethos of the times to keep a woman
trapped in a glass box—at best as stolen treasure. This way she
could be looked at; she could also be displayed. What she could
not be was autonomous; she could not live her own life. She was
a prisoner. Holding someone captive like this in turn just conjures up the exercise of power.

The woman in the story then compels both sultans to have
their way with her while the spirit is sleeping. What the sultan
sees as faithlessness can also be seen as cunning, an attempt just
to stay alive.

A man can think whatever he likes, but ultimately he cannot break a woman's spirit. This sentiment is articulated in a sen-
tence by the trapped and violated girl, "The monster doesn't
realize that the will of women cannot be controlled by any one."[9]

In other words, the power of women is something that
has to be reckoned with. It would be more helpful to give up
the mutual attempts at grasping and outwitting one another,

the duty to be faithful which is not abided by, and to have a real relationship.

We come to a similar conclusion when we relate the story to the level of intrapsychic events. Despite all Scheherban's attempts to keep his feminine side under control, the female always escapes and forces him to submit to her.

Overpowering another person, controlling her, isolating her, locking her up only call for the exercise of more power—the thirst for power and cunning as a way of cancelling out this dominance. But since a woman's physical strength is inadequate for such a struggle, and her social position does not lend any protection, cunning seems like a promising way of putting a stronger person or someone in a position of power out of action. That these women are all cunning shows that they still resist and also that they are clever. In order to be cunning one has to be capable of anticipating what someone else is thinking of doing. One has to be able to fantasize, even about evil. In addition, one has to know one's own shadows, one's own dark sides. The sultans' wives, who have a good time in their foridden encounters with slaves, know their own dark sides well.

That in this context Scheherban and Schahseman speak of the infidelity of women is understandable, but only at a superficial level. In actual fact, it is not possible to be true to someone or to misuse their trust if there is no trust there, when the only thing present is controlling behavior that manifests itself in the attempt to exert power and make them submit them to your will. Scheherban and Schahseman do no understand the signs of the time: Their wives are not listened to; they are killed. The crisis is not seen as a possibility for changing something in the relationship; instead even more power is brought to bear on the women—power that is deadly. The behavior that caused the problems in the first place is intensified, but this does not solve the problems.

Obviously such behavior patterns still exist today and are no less brutal, even if physical deaths do not always result. In this context I am thinking of people who are "untrue" to their partners. The "guilty" party is never given the opportunity to explain what has actually happened and what the state of affairs actually means. He or she is forever after labeled as a person who has cheated, someone who has to be kept under control, who has earned mistrust, who is always guilty. Under such circumstances the other person simply exerts control, playing more and more power games, and trust and love are less and less in evidence.

In the framing story, this cycle is interrupted by the appearance of Scheherezade. She knows what fate holds in store but trusts herself enough to avert it. With her courage and her trust in her own capabilities, she breaks through this deadly circle of power. She imposes no conditions—that in itself would be a kind of power play—as a real woman probably would; she does not say, "If you improve, then I'm going to deal with you differently." She simply does deal differently with the sultan, and because she behaves this way, he is able to change. But Scheherezade is a very special woman. She knows lots of books; she has an astonishing memory and has learned stories by heart. She is considered educated and wise, and she is very courageous.

A new relationship between man and woman begins: Scheherazade tells stories, and the king listens As the introduction to the framing story has shown, these are stories that teach us how to live. They are nourishment for the soul. To be sure, Scheherazade lives under a death threat, but she risks implementing what it is that she has to offer, and ultimately she is successful, after a thousand and one nights.

In this she would not however have been successful if the king had not listened, had not opened up a little bit. He too has to yield his dominating attitude toward women and adopt a new way of being, possibly because Scheherezade has come of her own free will.

In this short passage it is also clear that Sheherezade and her father, the vizier, have a very special relationship. The daughter is mindful of her father's concerns, and the father loves his daughter. As far as the sultan is concerned, women do not have any reason for existing, other than as sexual objects. On the other hand, there is a realm in which their existence is thoroughly confirmed—that of the relationship between daughters and fathers. The vizier, who is a governmental official, is also an important male representative of the regime. But this alternative connection corresponds only to a father–daughter relationship, not to that of partners.

Scheherezade succeeds in conveying a new image of women to the sultan: woman as a wise, clever, educated, helpful being. She also manages to involve him in a relationship—and in this subsists her cunning. They have sex, and they communicate via fairy stories. These stories however avert the sultan from killing, from having to be destructive.

So what role in this recovery story—or the story of accessing a new way of life—does the fairy tale "Ali Baba and the Forty Thieves" play?

How to Deal
with Poverty

Once upon a time in the land of Churaran in Persia there lived
two brothers. The older brother, Kasim, was rich and cruel. The younger,
Ali Baba, had taken a poor young woman as his wife and moreover, since
he did not know how to economize, what little he had possessed soon
became even less. Finally all their worldly possessions consisted of only a
roof over their heads, a donkey, and a slave named Mardschana, a young
woman with a pleasing appearance and a good head on her shoulders.

What was Ali Baba to do? After long consideration he finally decided to sell Mardschana as well. But she said to him, "Master, please don't
sell me. What little money you will get for me will soon have run through
your fingers and then you'll be in an even worse predicament than you
are now. Instead you should take the donkey into the mountains and col-
lect firewood there. You will be able to sell it at market."

Ali Baba liked this idea. The very next morning he took his ax and
wended his way into the mountains with his donkey. He worked there the
whole day, then loaded the wood onto the donkey which carried it to the
town bazaar. That evening a few gold pieces jingled in Ali Baba's purse.

From that day on Ali Baba earned a meager livelihood collecting firewood and had no more worries.

We are introduced to two brothers in the opening few passages of the story. One is rich and avaricious, the other poor, starry-eyed and noble. The story is concerned principally with Ali Baba who plunges deeper and deeper into poverty. The story addresses the issue of how to put a stop to this poverty and also how to rectify the inequality between the two brothers so that they are in a comparable position.

The story deems people impoverished when they have no more enthusiasm for life, expressed either as a lack of money or the lack of a means of subsistence. As is frequently pointed out here, they do not know how to economize, nor have they learned how to make use of the treasures that nature has put at their disposal and they are just as careless with everyday things.

At the same time, this material impoverishment represents an inner lack. There is no longer enough energy for living; the means of subsistence are lacking. Everything is in a state of decline and their whole way of life is all wrong.

He was at his wit's end and didn't know what to do. He saw no way of getting food and making a living, and yet he was a man of learning and understanding, of erudition and refinement.

They say to me, "Because of your wisdom you are like the moonlit night."

I say, "Leave me in peace with your speeches;

For wisdom doesn't mean anything without power.

Pawn me along with my wisdom, so too every book and pen for a single day's bread.

Look at the poor man's fate,

The life of the poor, how gloomy it is!

In the summer he lacks his daily bread,
In the winter he warms himself before the coal brazier.
The dogs in the street turn against him,
And every commoner scolds him;
If he complains about his lot,
Everyone bars their doors.
Such a fate only befalls a poor man,
It would be better if he were lying in his grave!" [10]

In this other, more elaborate version of the tale, Ali Baba is introduced as a man of wisdom. Because his wisdom does not pay, he looks around for work with his hands, something that will bring in the bread and butter.

Possibly the two brothers symbolize two different ways of conducting life: Ali Baba who concerns himself with knowledge and Kasim who pursues material wealth. The name "Ali Baba" could also point to this distinction. Although the story originally stems from Syria, the name "Ali Baba" is Turkish.[11]

In Islamic mysticism it is said that the esoteric wisdom of Muhammad the prophet was given to his cousin and step-son Ali ibn Abi Talib.[12] In the Bektashi Order, an Islamic brotherhood of mystics in thirteenth-century Turkey, the name "Baba" meant "spiritual leader," particularly among soldiers. The "Baba" was entrusted with preaching and care of the soul.[13] It may well be that Ali Baba is a person who belongs in the spiritual–mystical tradition and that here too he is impoverished. In this context, the impoverishment would indicate that he is lacking not only his daily bread but that his spirituality is also no longer nourishing.

If one considers his brother Kasim a man of the world, then one of the brothers is devoted exclusively to the world, the other brother just to the realm of the spirit. Both of them are one-sided, at least by today's standards.

What is still left to Ali Baba: a roof over his head, a donkey (a modest beast of burden), and a young slave woman with a pleasing appearance and a good head on her shoulders. (In the other version, however, Mardschana belongs to Ali Baba's brother. Ali Baba writes a poem about his suffering and in thinking about his predicament comes up with the idea of cutting wood himself.)

The shorter version of the story follows a well-established pattern: If you spare me then I can be of greater assistance to you (as, for example, in the story "The Golden Bird"[14]). In psychological terms, this represents the assertion that people—and in comparable stories also animals—with whom one establishes a relationship cannot be sold or killed. Instead one should accept their help. At the subject level, one could interpret this storyline to mean that there are aspects of the self that cannot just be hastily repressed or cleaved off in the hope that in the short term life will get easier. Instead, one needs to question what function these personality traits might serve.

From the story's inception, Mardschana, the slave, is represented as beautiful and clever. In contradistinction to the women in the framing story, this enslaved woman is true, beautiful, and at the same time very clever—already the image of woman has been somewhat transformed.

Mardschana is the only possession Ali Baba has left to sell. Mardschana says to him, however, that he has to stop making such rash decisions—the money would still just run through his fingers.

In saying this, Mardschana has introduced an important change into Ali Baba's life. She makes it clear to him that she is not simply a possession, but that she can be helpful to him. She gives him to understand that in actual fact, she is no longer a slave whom one can simply sell. She addresses the nature of her relationship. In so doing, she points out to him that in future, he cannot just look for easy solutions. Easy solutions might solve problems in the short term, but in the long-run they probably create greater problems. Ali Baba should tackle his problems head-on. Like Ali Baba, we too often try to solve problems with all kinds of piecemeal solutions, so that our life conditions do not really change and the old problems keep reappearing.

In this context, I recall the story of a couple who had little in common any more and were having considerable difficulties with their relationship. These fundamental problems would flare up in the context of acute everyday problems. It bothered the wife, for example, that her husband pursued various free-time activities with great regularity and in so doing, "used up" the time for their communal life. Following every discussion that ensued, the husband, who wanted to avoid a major conflict, agreed to give up his activities. This he then did, but in so doing felt depressed and listless, and the "together time" became a torture. He wondered to himself what else he could give up to feel better about things.

In such situations, and also in the case of Ali Baba, it has nothing to do with giving up more in order to keep one's head above water. It has to do with reconfiguring the situation in order to bring about a long-term change.

Ali Baba is supposed to chop wood and sell it, wood that is to be used to make fire and obtain warmth so that food can be prepared. To be sure, cutting wood is not just about Ali Baba earning a livelihood with his own hands, nor about working hard so that one stroke takes care of all his needs. He has to learn to economize. The longer version of the story also stipulates that Ali Baba works outdoors, that he heads off into the mountains through impassable terrain, that he tries new paths, and that he works at securing a material that transforms cold into warmth and the raw into the cooked. In so doing, he also transforms his life.

In the abbreviated version of the story, Mardschana gives Ali Baba some advice, but in the other version he comes upon the idea himself after having considered the situation in a poem. It also becomes clear to him what his qualities are and that they will not transform themselves into sustenance. In the end, he declares that he is really bone-weary.

What at first seems to be a contradiction is in fact not one.

If one takes Mardschana to be a psychological aspect of Ali Baba, then she embodies an energetic female *anima* that believes in the perpetuation of life, that has ideas. This side could be animated by a conversation with a woman who possesses some of these characteristics. It might also be evoked by Ali Baba plainly confronting his situation and admitting his feelings of helplessness, as he does in his poem.

Mardschana is a woman who belongs to an enslaved class, but who is nonetheless clever. It is impressive that Ali Baba trusts her so much that he is able to take advice even from her. On the other hand, perhaps he is already so deeply distressed that any advice would be welcome. It is, however, also conceivable that Mardschana has frequently given good pieces of advice and that her wisdom has been proven in the past. In any case, she knows all about everyday life and she knows people. Ali Baba's own wife does not know any better than he how to economize, so she cannot give him any help, nor does his relationship with her generate any new ideas on the subject. Mardschana's advice can thus be understood as advice from a woman who lives under other conditions and who embodies the attitude that life should only be given up for lost when it truly is lost. She embodies the aspect of hope; she believes that life can be shaped and that life can also be changed for the better.

In any event, the outcome is that the necessities of life are taken care of and that life becomes possible again. Ali Baba now travels back and forth from the mountains to the bazaar.

Mardschana's advice gets him out of the house and outside of the security of the city. He enters a wild, probably undeveloped mountain region. From a psychological point of view, Ali Baba enters a life situation that is new, difficult, and characterized by unruly feelings.

The mountains appear as a realm of the unforeseeable. It is an area where people live who, for various reasons, have moved out of the city. It is an unprotected zone. Here one encounters dangers and people who are excluded from everyday life.

In listening to the advice of his serving slave, Ali Baba also broadens his social horizon. From a psychological perspective, he accesses sides of himself that are ranked "inferior" and beneath his level. Only Mardschana's cleverness places her above a typical slave.

New ways of behaving enable us to access new spaces for living. These spaces are generally unprotected when the impulse to open ourselves to them stems from the enslaved part of our psyche. Progress and risk imply one another. Whenever ordered life generates feelings of poverty and insufficiency, then we have to turn to our enslaved sides, our shadow sides. In so doing, it becomes clear which aspects of life have been hitherto excluded. We learn something about the things that are responsible for the fact that we are suffocating in our habitual ways of doing things. Yet our enslaved sides do not always behave as beneficently as Mardschana in the story. She is exceptionally helpful.

The Thieving Shadow

One day when he was busy cutting wood, there suddenly appeared in the distance a cloud of dust that approached rapidly. Soon he could make out a band of riders, wild and dangerous-looking fellows with sabers and daggers that filled him with terror. Ali Baba quickly drove his donkey into the undergrowth and climbed the nearest tree, whose thick crown hid him from the wild bunch—forty men in all.

And it was under just this tree that the riders stopped, jumped off their horses, threw their saddlebags over their shoulders, and walked toward a nearby rocky outcrop that was covered in thick brush.

Then another man—judging by his clothing and his behavior he must have been their leader—appeared and called out, "Open sesame!" At exactly the same moment a door in the rocks opened, admitted the riders, and then closed behind them again.

After a while the men emerged from the rocks again and Ali Baba had the opportunity to take a closer look at them. By their wild appearance, their bearded faces, and their dark, ominous looks, he concluded that it must be none other than the terrible robber band that had long been terrorizing the area. So this was where they had the cave for hiding their loot!

The robbers fastened their now empty bags onto their saddles, mounted their horses, and disappeared as quickly as they had come.

From an intrapsychic point of view, when people become increasingly impoverished, then generally it involves more than having the wrong attitude toward life. Almost always there are forces at work that deprive them of what does not belong to them.

If we are under the impression that we have less and less energy to deal with life, that we get less and less pleasure from what we do and from things that used to be thoroughly satisfying, then it is time to go in search of whatever it is that is depleting us, the forces that are depriving our consciousness of control.

They appear then, these forty thieves!

If one examines the title of this story, then it is patently obvious that somehow and at some point Ali Baba has to come into conflict with the forty thieves. In truth, this is no trivial matter, since these thieves are threatening not only by virtue of their number,but also because they look wild and dangerous.

They arouse fear—a sign that Ali Baba feels threatened by some great danger that he cannot confront. For the time being, his only recourse is to hide in the tree. Thus protected, he can spy out the robbers' secret; he can observe them without their being aware that they are being observed, and without giving them cause to stage any opposition.

Just as the cutting of firewood had for the time being alleviated Ali Baba's greatest needs, a tree now gives him protection. The tree is shown here serving its salvational, motherly function. In the face of a threatening situation, Ali Baba withdraws to a place where he feels protected and has an overview of the situation. (He could have simply hidden himself behind a rock.)

And what does this all mean, if we regard the story as symbolic? It means that we are afraid to face the battle with our powerful thieving sides. We flee—into the branches of a tree.

We feel threatened. First of all, we observe what is causing the threat. The picture becomes clear. We no longer have vague, indeterminate fears, but rather a specific fear of the robbers. We are probably also afraid of loosing our lives—a threat indicated by daggers and swords, attributes that these men wield so terrifyingly.

The flight into the tree might then be the image of our immediately withdrawing to a position that gives us protection—perhaps to a person whom we see as unshakable, like a tree. Perhaps we take stock of our life: life is now seen as a tree that has thrived up until now. We remind ourselves that life, like a tree, has roots, that were hitherto always protected—that just as we are protected by the roof of a house, so too are the roots protected by the crown of the tree. Perhaps we also remind ourselves that in good times as in bad, a tree is able to grow.

This notion of a tree as a symbol of human growth in sunshine or in storms also embodies the idea that there are always safe havens, places that protect us. Just the idea that a tree grows, and thinking of how it grows, might be comforting to us when we find ourselves in situations in which our ego is threatened. These ideas and thoughts convey the impression that life is not just dependent on us alone. And this thought may well be able to protect us.

We can protect ourselves by simply hiding and not wanting to see or hear anything. This self-defense might be necessary on occasion. However, a protected position from which we have an overview of the situation allows confrontation to occur at some later date.

When we withdraw from something out of fear and simply avoid the things that frighten us, then we become ever more afraid. We no longer even recognize just what it is that makes us afraid. In our fear, we fantasize about it so that it seems very dangerous. In so doing, the frightening situation becomes more and more frightening. By climbing up the tree, Ali Baba makes sure he is safe, but at the same time he keeps the robbers in view.

And it is under this very tree that the robbers then stop. This image makes clear that the robbers also belong to Ali Baba, or at least to the tree that he has chosen as his own. They come nearer and he can thus keep them in eyesight.

Not counting their leader, there are forty robbers. The number forty expresses their superior numbers. In Islamic mysticism the number forty is often "identical with 'multitude' and seems to refer to an indeterminate quantity"[15]. Forty is also the number of patience. It is forty days that are significant to the Sufis, as they were to Jesus in the desert: that number of days represents a time of preparation, a time of confrontation which is then superseded by a new life situation, and the beginning of one's real life's work. The wandering of the Israelites in the desert lasted forty years before they arrived in the promised land. The number forty is a sacred number, a number that indicates that an inner goal has been attained. According to Annemarie Schimmel, for European Sufis in Turkey the "Forty" among the group of saints assume a special position.[16] In Turkey there are even place names that are associated with their presence.

Is it conceivable that behind the forty robbers there were originally concealed forty saints? And were this the case, what could have transpired that would have transformed forty saints into robbers? Even if we do not want to pursue this train of thought, it should still be kept in the back of our minds.

In the first place, the forty robbers refer to a multitude, but also to the fact that this group constitutes a closed totality. Examined at the subject level, for Ali Baba this means that he urgently needs to confront his robber sides, but also that he *can* confront them. Now is a good time to take care of matters so that he can subsequently get on with his life's work.

The Robbers

Robbers represent the thieving sides within a society, but also within us. These thieving sides are not something that we usually show openly. We are afraid of them and try to keep them in check. In other words, we try not to act openly in a thieving way. For most of us, our thieving sides are those aspects of our personality that we cannot easily reconcile with our own image of ourselves. So we deny them or project them onto other people. We see the thieving sides much more clearly in others than we do in ourselves. Our own thieving sides lie for the most part "in shadow," but they affect our lives when we try to ignore them. Thieving traits are also our opportunistic, aggressive, and destructive sides. In this tale, aggression, greed, and cunning are united in the figure of the robbers. Robbers do not reflect on things very much, they try to get what they want, and what they want is to enrich themselves. They kill whatever gets in their way and count on the stupidity and overly naive sense of trust of human beings. They outwit people whenever they can.

Our thieving shadow sides are at work whenever we enrich ourselves at someone else's expense—when we consciously present ourselves as benefactors—or at the very least, do not admit our own intentions to enrich ourselves. But it does not just have to be material advantage that is at stake: when we pretend that other people's ideas are our own and over time forget that they do not belong to us, then our thieving side is operating to its own advantage. Robber shadows are also at work when we undermine people and make deprecating remarks about them behind their backs. Generally we do this quite explicitly, saying "Far be it from me to judge, but . . ."

The thieving shadow can also play a role in our relationships with the self: we rob ourselves of many of our opportunities in life because other life possibilities seem more likely to earn us power, prestige, or money. Whether they really can is another matter. A thieving shadow is also at work when we are unable to give, when we are careful to keep everything for ourselves, when we are wholly caught up in the principle of "having" or possessing. Even if we do not readily admit it, the thieving shadow plays a role in many aspects of life.

Most people feel ambivalent toward the robbers in the fairy tale. Naturally the robbers are represented as immoral monsters, and of course everyone is happy at the end of the story when they find out that the robbers have been defeated and their handiwork exposed. But secretly we also admire them. As it turns out during the course of the story, this conspiratorial bunch also has its rules: they are men who seize opportunities, who admit their greed and take whatever they want. And they fascinate us. In identifying with the fairy-tale robbers, our own thieving sides can revive somewhat, particularly since we know that in the end they will be defeated. We don't need to be afraid that we won't be able to rid ourselves of these thieving aspects of the self.

So Ali Baba encounters his thieving shadow. Since there are so many robbers it can be assumed that this thieving shadow is part of a collective problem—in fact this is something that the framing story alludes to at the outset. Ali Baba, like all fairy-tale heros and heroines, solves not only his own personal problem, but in representing the personal, he also works out a problem that concerns all of us at a certain point in time.

It is the local robbers then who are up to their dirty tricks; these are the ones who are causing problems in Ali Baba's neighborhood. However, he has recognized them; he knows what the problem is, and it frightens him. But he is also surprised that he has never noticed the doorway in the rock wall that was covered by thick undergrowth. He also now knows an exciting secret, namely that this is where the robbers have their cave, the hiding-place for their treasure. And that the door really opens to the formula, "Open sesame!"

Something happens to Ali Baba that happens to all of us when we are confronted by our own shadow sides: we become afraid, but we also sense that something new is on the verge of opening up. When the robbers have disappeared Ali Baba breathes a sigh of relief, just like we do when an acute threat has passed.

Hidden Riches

Ali Baba let out a sigh of relief. But instead of beating a quick retreat he wanted to find out whether the rock would also obey his command.

"Open sesame!" he called just as he had heard the leader of the robber band do. And lo and behold, the door opened silently and he stepped inside. Once he had entered the cave, his eyes nearly popped out of his head at the sight of all the treasure that the robbers had amassed: whole mountains of gold pieces, precious stones as big as a fist, fabric from India and China, pearls like the sands of the sea . . . Ali Baba paced the entire cave, his eyes getting wider and wider. Such treasures he would never have dared to dream of!

Ali Baba now shows courage. Through his encounter with the forty robbers, something has been awakened in him: his own brave thieving side. He wants to know whether he too can open the door—and he finds that he can.

In order for us to be able to conjure up the treasures that Ali Baba discovers so that we too can revel in the wealth and sensuality of the story, I am including the longer version of the text:

Now seeing the door open, Ali Baba entered the cave; but barely had he stepped over the threshold when the door closed behind him… But when he thought of the words "Sesame, open your door!," the fear and terror that had overcome him abated, and he said to himself, "What do I care if the door closes. I know the secret that will open it." So he went in a little way, and since he was under the impression that the cave was a single dark room, he was absolutely amazed when he spied a huge, lighted hall made of marble that was adorned with high pillars and decorated in splendor, and laid out in the hall was everything by way of food and drink that one's heart could desire. From there he stepped into a second hall that was even larger and more spacious than the first. In it he saw the most wonderful wares coupled with the rarest jewels, the glimmer of which charmed the eye and whose description no one could do justice. There lay an abundance of pure solid gold bars, and other things of fine silver; vast numbers of dinars and dirhem coins; all in piles like mounds of sand and pebbles, too many for either counting or estimating. After he had looked around for a while in this wondrous hall, yet another door opened before him. He went through it and came into a third hall, that was even more splendid and beautiful than the second. It was filled with the finest garments from all the regions and countries of the earth. In it there were fabrics made of the finest, most expensive cotton, and clothes made of silk and the most magnificent brocades in the world. There was in fact not a single type of fabric that was not to be found in this room. There was fabric from Syria's fertile plains and from Africa's farthest reaches, from China and the Industal, from Nubia and the Middle East. And beyond this room, Ali Baba entered the hall of precious stones, which was the largest and most fantastic of all. It contained more pearls and jewels than one could either grasp or count, hyacinths and emeralds, turquoise and topaz, and mountains of pearls; one saw agates lying there side by side with bits of coral. Finally, Ali Baba went into the hall of spices, of incense and perfume, and this was the last of the halls. Here he found things so delicate, and made of all kinds of the finest things. The scent of aloe wood

and musk wafted up; amber and zibet radiated forth in all their beauty;
the magic of rosewater and nadd (a perfume made of amber, musk and
aloe wood) filled the air; a hint of frankincense and saffron rose in an
exquisite fragrance; sandalwood lay about like cords of firewood; aromat-
ic roots had been cast down like brushwood as though someone had had
no need of them any more. Ali Baba was transfixed by the sight of this
immeasurable wealth; his senses deceived him and his reason left him. He
stood there for a while, completely overpowered and transported . . .[17]

If we submit ourselves to the images presented in this
excerpt, then it is possible to forget for a moment that we are in
a robbers' lair. We are much more likely to get the impression
that we are in the land of Cockaigne, in an Oriental bazaar
where the most beautiful things in the world have been
amassed. Everything on earth that is valuable seems to be stored
here. It is an image of the beauty of the world. The objects
appeal to our senses: we want to taste the food, to wonder at the
gold and the precious stones, to touch the fabrics, and to breath
in the scent of the spices.

We encounter a wonderful treasure, even if it is under the
stewardship of the robbers. In this more elaborate version, however, it is stated, "This treasure must have been present even
before the robbers stumbled upon it."[18] In other words, sometime, somehow, the treasure must have fallen into the hands of
the robbers.

Whereas beforehand Ali Baba was paralyzed by fear, now he
is "completely overpowered and transported" by the treasure
which presents itself to him. A world of glitter, perfume, wealth,
and beauty is opened up to him, and seizes him to his very core.

The thieving side in him opens him up to overwhelming
riches. He is beset by greed, the hunger for power, for wealth. In
other words, he is seized by a completely egocentric impulse, an

aggressive grasping that does not consider the consequences for other people; it is a desire which opens his heart to the treasure.

Ali Baba is reminiscent of a person whose day-to-day existence is very modest, who "achieves" little but who is unconsciously driven by a desire for wealth, prestige, and power. Of course, if we were to question someone like this about it, they would say that such traits are despicable. If however, they were then to encounter their own thieving shadow, the shadow that has deprived them of so much, and they were to become aware of their thieving tendencies, they might even beome robbers themselves when the hidden treasures of life's possibilities are opened up to them. If they admit to such ambition and such feelings of power, then they might suddenly find out just what potential their life harbors and what riches might be accessible to them.

In this context, I am reminded of a woman client who exhibited all kinds of inhibitions. She barely expressed a single desire, and did not dare to accept anything that she was offered. She considered everyone else base and ambitious; only she herself was above this. She considered other people greedy and judged them for this. Yet in her studied lack of aggression, she came across as being very demanding; in fact, everyone who came into contact with this depressive woman felt bound to discern every wish in her eyes and to make the decisions that she herself would not make. She seemed demanding, aroused aggression, yet gave the people around her the feeling that she was quite "ordinary." This example illustrates the fact that particularly when there seems to be no trace of these thieving sides, they can nonetheless be in effect and can signal a problem that needs to be dealt with.

This same woman dreamed the following dream: "I have a pirate ship under my command. I sail along the Cote d'Azur in the pirate ship and plunder and steal whatever I like. It feels great." In dreaming this, it became clear to the woman that she too had wishes and longings that she would like to fulfill without too much exertion.

There are people who for egocentric reasons—perhaps to gain power and prestige—seek wisdom. They practice meditation in order to become more successful and more significant than other people, not in order to come into contact with something that is larger than themselves or to feel grounded. In the language of the fairy tale, such people act with thieving intent. Yet at some point on this robber course, they may be affected by whatever it is that they want to "have." Then it becomes a matter no longer of just wanting to have and hoard something in order to wield power; it becomes an issue of introducing what appears before one as a vision of utopia into everyday life. Otherwise one just stays a robber.

Ali Baba is disillusioned by the fear of that which makes the robbers terrifying. It shakes him out of the state of intoxication in which he obviously finds himself.

The Fascination
with Beauty

But what have the robber sides opened up to Ali Baba?
First of all, they convey to him the formula "Open sesame!," so
that he intuits that even apparently locked doors can open. In
the longer version of the story the formula is "Sesame, open
your door!" The explanation for this is as follows: "In Babylon-
ian-Assyrian conjuring formulas, the sesame plant was cited as a
means of undoing magic spells. Even today the Arabs still regard
the sesame oil press as the home of spirits. In the formula,
"Sesame, open your door!," *sesame* (in Arabic *sumsum*) is presumably just a magic or cabalistic word. "Open the door!" really
should say, "Open the door for . . ."[19]

In keeping with this explanation, it is not sesame per se that
is important, but rather the connection between the robbers or
at least the robber leader, and the spirit that is capable of opening the door. This in turn would point to the great power that is
contained in these robbers—power not only over people, but
also power over spirits.

In Greek mythology, sesame and honey are also used to make the so-called "mülloi,"[20] images of the female genitals, in which honey is conceived of as the "purest mother's milk."[21] This association suggests the interpretation that the entrance way in the rock might well have something to do with "sesame," in other words that it might well be the womb of a female, motherly vessel, and also that the cave is natural.

The cave in the mountain has the character of a vessel; it conceals something. The concealing cave as part of the mountain is the natural form of the temple and so too of the house,[22] analogous with the mother's womb, which is also the first home of a child. According to Neumann, the cave lying in the mountain also belongs to the dark territory of the earth's underworld. The cave not only can provide shelter, but also can contain great wealth, which it may withhold. In this case, it does not relinquish any of its treasures, and instead becomes a place of death.

Together with the cave, the entrance, or the doorway in general, is one of the main symbols of the Great Goddess. And I think that the formula "Open sesame!" also alludes to this. The robbers have access to the Great Mother. The fullness of life expressed by the Great Mother is available to them. They have an entry way to the feminine, even if they steal from it. They simply hoard the treasures, but they cannot initiate the birth process. This in turn would suggest that the robber sides work in the service of holding fast, antithetical to the notion of containing, which holds in order to give.

When we consider the images sequentially, then the treasures in the mountain might be compared with the captured woman in the glass box.

First of all, the treasures distinguish themselves on the basis of their great beauty. If one takes a closer look at them, one finds that many of them spring from the female realm of life—the food, the fabrics, the precious stones, the fragrances, the spices.

They all have something to do with the world of sensual pleasure. All these treasures are reminiscent of Eros, the experience of beauty, but they are hoarded in the cave and are not yet able to be transported back to real life. This may be the reason why Ali Baba is so poor and why the robbers have gained such great significance: the female assets are hoarded. The robbers are powerful, rich, but the amassed beauty cannot be introduced to other people. Under these conditions, the fullness of life cannot be evoked. Nothing new is born.

To the Sufi however, beauty represents the beauty of God. It creates love, since love without contemplation—and contemplation stems from love—would be meaningless.[23] The statement "Ali Baba was transfixed by the sight of this immeasurable wealth, he lost his senses; he stood there for a while completely overwhelmed and enraptured" alludes to mystical emotion.

It is thus conceivable that Ali Baba is struck by a wealth of life-possibilities, that he acquires new hope and in so doing, also feels reinvigorated. These new life-possibilities might arise in connection with Eros and sensual intoxication, but his emotion in response to the overwhelming beauty might also suggest that he is having a mystical experience.

The forty robbers on the other hand, might be conceived of as corrupted saints, in that they keep for themselves objects that should represent the beauty of God. They no longer allow these objects to be distributed among mankind; they hoard them rather than letting them take effect for themselves or others. This then would be the thieving aspect in this religious interpretation: accumulating things rather than letting them affect us.

An Altered Life

But fear of the robbers soon shook him out of his reverie. They might be back any minute, and if they found him here that would be the end of him.

Quickly he took as many bags of gold as he could carry and gave the command, "Open sesame!" Outside he loaded the bags of gold onto the donkey and arranged a covering of firewood over the top so that no one would discover his priceless load. Then he raced home, hoping that the robbers would not notice anything and that they would not follow him.

Once safely at home, he barred the door so as to be sure that no one would come in unexpectedly. Then to his wife's complete amazement, he shook the gold onto the floor so that it jangled. His wife was beside herself with happiness, but she was also afraid. Only when Ali Baba assured her that he had taken just the smallest fraction of the robbers' horde, so that they were unlikely to notice anything, did her fears subside. Then she got to the business of counting the dinars.

"At this rate you won't be done by this evening," said Ali Baba. "And we still have to hide the money. I think the best thing to do would be to bury it in the garden."

Fear of the robbers brings Ali Baba back down to earth—he knows he is in danger. Quite level-headedly he still recalls the formula, carefully hides the bags full of treasure, making sure that nothing falls out. He has become cautious—he now knows about his own robber sides as well as those in other people. Fear also drives him home.

Yet in bringing home the gold dinars, visible signs of change become apparent. Such an event cannot be concealed.

When people permit fantasies connected with their shadow sides to come to life, they suddenly sense what longings they harbor, and the life-possibilities that are expressed in utopian dreams. These fantasies then transform themselves into a new life force—they become more lively, more energetic. They are indeed afraid of the possibilities which they see; they are afraid of the greed which overcomes them and which does not leave them a single peaceful moment. Yet they cannot undo such experiences, nor can they hide them.

And so Ali Baba brings home gold dinars as evidence that something decisive has happened. Money represents new energy, which allows for a better standard of living. Gold signifies that this energy is very valuable—since gold is the symbol of the eternal/indestructible and points to the fact that this increase in wealth is associated with an experience of the eternal/indestructible.

Ali Baba's wife, who now assumes the role of intermediary with the world, ensures that the great event also has real consequences. She shows that the associated problems can be worked out; she is beside herself with joy, but also with fear.

Joy and fear are the emotions that we experience when we become aware of a shadow realm. We fear these sides; otherwise we would not have suppressed them so long. We also sense however, that something alive is bursting open, that something important is happening when we rediscover these sides—and about this we are happy.

Ali Baba plays down his fear of the robbers—they won't notice anything, he tells his wife. Still he thinks he might be able to hide everything, to bury the gold in his garden. If one interprets the garden as the realm which, as the symbolic tradition would have it, concerns the "personal cultivation of erotic relationships," one might imagine that the experience with the rock has reinvigorated his relationship with his wife—and that this might actually satisfy Ali Baba.

The Principle of Having;
Or, Envy

But because his wife absolutely had to know just how rich they were, she quickly ran over to the wife of the wealthy Kasim in order to borrow a bushel scale. "What sort of grain are those poor paupers ever going to weigh?" wondered Kasim's wife to herself when her sister-in-law made her request. And out of sheer curiosity she secretly poured some wax into the bottom of the scale before she lent it out.

While Ali Baba dug a pit in the garden, his wife measured out fully ten bushels of gold dinars; then together they buried the gold in the garden.

The very same day Kasim's wife got her scale back. She turned it over and lo! Stuck in the wax was a gold piece.

"So that's it!" she shrieked and ran straight to her husband. "Your brother has been pleading poverty when in reality he weighs his gold with a bushel scale."

Kasim, who had always been possessed by stinginess, greed, and envy, could not sleep a wink that night. He tossed and turned. He knew that he would never sleep peacefully again if he did not find out where his brother had gotten the money.

So directly after the morning prayers he went and knocked on Ali Baba's door. Ali Baba welcomed his older brother in a friendly and fitting way, but Kasim got straight to the point and called him a hypocrite and a liar who had just been feigning poverty. "I know that you have to weigh the gold with a bushel scale if you want to know how much you even have. Here is the proof!" And he waved in front of his face a dinar that his wife had picked out of the wax on the scale. "Either you tell me where you got the money or I'm going to inform the judge about you."

"I'd be happy to tell you everything, brother," said Ali Baba, who didn't know any other way out of the situation. And he reported truthfully what had happened to him the previous day. In fact, at Kasim's insistence, he even described the exact route to the robber's den. "But I don't advise you to challenge fate and go there," he warned. "Better that I share everything with you, than that I knowingly expose you to danger and that you fall into the terrible hands of the robbers." But Kasim just laughed at him. "You idiot, do you honestly think that I would pass up the opportunity to become a hundred times richer?"

With these words he ran off with all haste to town where he bought all the donkeys he could lay his hands on, so that pretty soon people started to think that he wanted to do the donkey drivers out of a job. And out of pure excitement, he could not sleep a wink this night. As soon as dawn came, he took his caravan into the mountains and soon found the rocky outcrop that Ali Baba had described to him.

"Open sesame!" he called, and the door actually opened and let him inside. When he looked around the cave and saw how much was lying about he was glad he had bought so many donkeys, since not even these would be able to carry it away all at once. But what to take first? As though possessed, he laid sacks full of gold and precious stones ready at the entrance; he carried great chests, lamps and priceless fabrics. In his greed and obsession, he completely forgot the world around him; he just grasped and clutched at things. Finally, he thought that he had enough for one day and that it was time to carry everything outside and load up the animals.

But alas! Thinking the whole time only of his riches, he had forgotten the name of the rock door. All he could recall was that it was some *grain or other and he tried each of them in turn as they occurred to him: "Oats, open up!" Then, "Open barley!" "Open up, wheat!"*

He named one type of grain after the other. Only one could he not recall—sesame.

The rock stayed shut, and in desperation Kasim started to cry out for help. Too late, he bemoaned, to listen to his brother's advice.

Even greater was his terror when he heard hoof-beats outside. The robbers had returned. They discovered the donkeys outside the cave and of course they immediately realized what was going on.

"Open sesame!" commanded the leader of the robbers fiercely. The rock door opened and Kasim stormed out of the cave, seeking safety in flight. But he did not make it two steps when the robbers felled him with their knives. Then they dragged the body into the cave, leaving it right by the entrance as a warning to anyone who might venture to try the same thing.

Having done this, they drove the donkeys away, carried the treasure back to its place, and added their latest bounty. Moments later the only evidence that the robber band had ever been there was a dust cloud receding in the distance. The surroundings were as abandoned and devoid of life as before.

The principle of having—embodied in this fairy tale in its most extreme form, namely that of the robbers—begins to take effect. Ali Baba's wife wants to know exactly how rich they are, probably so that she can get even more excited about it. At the same time, Kasim's wife suspects that her poor sister-in-law might perhaps own something that she does not have.

This principle of having is not only manifest in the declared aims of the robbers, it is in fact quite widespread. The most impressive example is that of Kasim, who for his part is basically a true robber. He is possessed by "avarice, greed, and envy." He is driven by thoughts of rivalry—he will not forgo an opportunity to become a hundred times richer than his brother.

We should bear in mind that at the beginning of the story, Kasim was depicted as the brother who became richer and richer, and Ali Baba as the poor one, who only got poorer. At the beginning of the story it was not clear whether Kasim was simply luckier or whether there was a preexisting state of rivalry between the brothers. In the meantime, it has become clear: Kasim is envious and avaricious; it would be all right with him if he were the richer of the two and Ali Baba hardly had anything left to live on. In a situation in which thievery has gained such an upper hand, the relationship between the brothers becomes characterized not by brotherly helpfulness, but rather by thievery, the desire to outdo each other, to overreach each other. The greed, the desire to have more, to own more, stands in the foreground; relationship values are not cultivated, are unimportant. It is not only the robber band that makes the countryside unsafe: Kasim, the older brother of Ali Baba, is similarly motivated by this thieving behavior. And as the brother of Ali Baba, he embodies a thieving side that is far closer to Ali Baba's consciousness than the thieving side represented by the robber band.

In the figure of Kasim, the story once again makes plain just how a thieving shadow works. Kasim is consumed with envy; he loses sleep, grows impatient, can barely wait for morning. The longer version goes on to say that he and his wife spent the entire night in "a wretched state of mind, so heavy was their sorrow, so bitter their sadness."[24] They behave as though they have suffered a terrible loss, and this great sorrow has to be averted the next day, without delay, cost what it may. Gone is the conviction of being the one of two brothers who has more—therefore, probably also the feeling of being more valuable than the other.

This suggests a comparison with the sultan's reaction in the framing story when he sees that his wife loves a slave, or with the fact that both sultans are looking for someone who has had an even worse time with women than they have had so that they can feel better about themselves. This, too, is robber behavior, when positive feelings of self-worth are derived from the knowledge that there are people in the world who are having a harder time of it than we are. It means that we always have to ensure ourselves that someone else is worse off. Regarded thus, envy is the emotion that signals that we have a poor way of confirming our own self-worth.

In terms of this fairy tale, an avaricious, greedy, envious person would be someone who was like an impermeable rock wall: he or she might well have treasures stored away, but they would not be accessible to others and would not play a role in the person's relationships. One could only hope that he or she might open up—"Open sesame!" in the best possible sense.

Kasim wants to seize the treasure, in the sense of stealing it. Already the haste in which he sets out and the circumspection with which he buys up so many donkeys suggest evil intent. In contradistinction to the experience of Ali Baba, Kasim lacks any sense of fear of the robbers. He himself is a robber and identifies with this thieving quality. Why then should he have anything to fear?

Once inside the cave, he also lacks a sense of amazement, a perception of the treasure in all its beauty. "In his greed and obsession he forgot the whole world around him, he seized and snatched at things." It is not the beauty of the objects that is important to him, but only the future wealth that will ensue. He is totally absorbed with his own wealth. Nor has he any sense of marvel that the door has opened, otherwise he would not have been cavalier with the magic formula which he has so quickly forgotten. We forget important things when fantasies and self-important ideas keep us occupied. Here it is clearly the *idée fixe* of wanting to have, the idea of wanting to have more than others, that determines his thinking. And so it is logical that he himself remains trapped as a prisoner of the cave. He is after all already so very obsessed, captured even, by the principle of having.

For Kasim the cave proves to be not a realm that harbors great treasure, but rather a place that brings death to him. The attitude embodied by Kasim does not permit access to its inner richness. One cannot simply steal from such a place.

When this thieving disposition has rendered many values defunct in daily life such that they have become unconscious in the life of the individual or in the life of the collective, then one cannot continue to practice the same attitudes that brought about this repression and splitting and hope to reintegrate the hidden treasures into life. For this one needs a fundamentally different *modus operandum.*

This new *modus operandum* is in part embodied by Ali Baba. We have dealt with Kasim as though he were a real life brother of Ali Baba. However, if we re-examine the story at the symbolic level, then Kasim can also be seen as representing a "shadow brother," a very closely related side of Ali Baba's "ego," one with which he feels strong kinship, but one that he has also differentiated himself from. From this perspective, Ali Baba would also have an avaricious, greedy, envious side. He too could and can enter into this sort of behavior.

Once he became aware of what treasure and what value lay there in the cave, Ali Baba might suddenly have felt the wild desire to fetch out considerably more. The conversation between Ali Baba and Kasim can thus be seen as a conversation with the self in which the better "ego" (Ali Baba) tries to get there in time to warn his thieving self. But in vain.

When we have an experience that enlivens us, an experience that is fulfilling, a door opens up that was hitherto closed. The hunger for this life experience can then get the upper hand: we want to have it again, whatever it may cost. We slip into thieving behavior unexpectedly. In so doing, we also become vulnerable to the robbers.

When a brother sets off on a journey in a fairy tale, it always means that someone has tried to solve a problem in a particular way. If he should die in the effort, then the particular behavior that he embodies dies too. Here it becomes unmistakably clear that the behaviors of envy, avarice, and greed cannot survive; they lead to death.

Female Solutions

Ali Baba waited two days for his brother's return, but the longer he waited the greater was his fear that the robbers had surprised Kasim in the cave. When he still had not returned on the third day, Ali Baba's terrible suspicion became almost a certainty. Finally he could stand it no longer and set off for the robbers' den. He approached very cautiously, avoiding every crackling branch. But the stillness around finally gave him a sense of security.

"Open sesame!" He called out the magic password. Oh! what horror! Right in the entrance to the cave lay the bloody corpse of his brother, proof that it does not pay to toy with robbers.

Ali Baba loaded the dead Kasim onto his donkey so that at least he could be given a decent burial and took a round-about route home. He didn't want to run into anyone.

At home he was still afraid that the robbers, having discovered the disappearance of the body, would follow his tracks and exact their terrible revenge.

In his distress, he confided in his clever slave, Mardschana. "Master, that's really horrible," said the young woman. "Don't tell anyone, don't breathe a single word. It would be best to let it be known that Kasim has died of a dreadful illness. And in order to be sure, make your sister-in-law your second wife. Then we'll all move into your brother's house."

Ali Baba followed Mardschana's advice word-for-word. He settled in the city, took over his brother's business and in one stroke he was a wealthy man.

Ali Baba has to take note consciously that his brother's undertaking has gone amiss. When we approach a thing from the wrong perspective, then afterwards we also have to be conscious of the fact that we went about things with the wrong attitude and accept that this attitude can no longer be revived. It has to be buried once and for all.

Of course, this tale also manifests the narrative features characteristic of the type of fairy story that has a rich brother and a poor brother, in which the rich brother is always greedy and avaricious, the impoverished one, very noble and helpful. In this sort of story, life is always perpetuated by the poor brother. This theme also plays a role in this particular story. Ali Baba thinks of his brother's welfare, not just about his wealth. If he too were avaricious and envious, he would be able to enjoy a certain malicious joy: he had forewarned him and now he has been punished. Ali Baba has not had to lift a finger; he does not have to feel the slightest twinge of guilt about it. But such thoughts are far from Ali Baba's mind. He is a man who, apart from thieving sides, has also developed the capacity for relationships. This quality is manifest in the fact that Ali Baba was willing to hand over half of his money to his brother. He does not derive his self-worth from wanting to have more than his brother, but rather from the fact that he is willing to share with his brother; he is brotherly.

However, the fate that befell his brother makes Ali Baba fearful. He is afraid of the robbers. Thinking at first that the robbers would not have noticed anything, he now becomes aware that one does not play around with these robber sides. He is in dire need and confides in his slave Mardschana. This means that at first he tries to downplay the danger of his own thieving sides, but then becomes so afraid of them that he seeks refuge in his slave. Regarded from the point of view of the subject level, he seeks refuge in his female side, in his own emotional being.

He cannot rid himself of the danger imposed by these robbers. Now that he no longer suppresses the fear, he suffers great distress. And when we suffer great distress, we search out a person to whom we can tell our troubles, someone who can give us some advice. The advice comes—already as in the beginning of the story—from the slave Mardschana.

Initially her advice is again that of concealment: Ali Baba should pretend Kasim has died a natural death and then marry Kasim's wife and take over everything that Kasim had owned.

From a psychological point of view, Mardschana's pronouncement is right: Kasim has died a natural death. Once a behavior like that embodied by Kasim has once and for all proved untenable, then one can simply let it die. That Kasim's entire worldly possessions are passed on to Ali Baba has to do with the fact that in the final analysis our shadow brother also belongs to us and embodies our other side. Often we lack imagination or energy because they are associated with our shadow aspect which we do not allow to coexist.

If we are able to face our shadow sides and can withstand the dilemmas in which we find ourselves and the contradictions that entangle us, then we can also have access to the energies and imaginative qualities that are linked to these sides. Naturally Mardschana advises Ali Baba to behave in the best way a brother of his time would have been expected to behave.

Significantly, "Ali Baba followed Mardschana's advice to the letter." Mardschana is thus also the one who takes over the leadership role in the struggle with the robbers.

Ali Baba allows someone to help him; he also trusts Mard-schana. We can assume for the moment that in Mardschana we are dealing with an actual servant who together with Ali Baba withstood the dangerous period. Naturally she could also be an inner helpful, albeit enslaved, *anima* figure. Since this too has to be brought to life through a relationship of one kind or another, I chose to interpret Mardschana here as a real, existing relation-ship–person. However, I will also keep referring to the fact that she represents the symbol of a psychic characteristic, and a fas-cinating one at that.

Outwitting the Robbers

Nor indeed did the robbers stay inactive. That the body had disappeared proved that there was someone else who knew both their hiding-place as well as the secret password. They spread out through the whole area in an effort to find the intruder. The bravest of them took on the most difficult assignment: to comb the city that lay in closest proximity to the cave. The leader of the robber band advised him to disguise himself as a merchant so as not to draw any attention to himself if he were to question people surreptitiously. This robber proved to be particularly sly and in no time he learned who had died recently and who had unexpectedly become rich as a result. More than that he did not need to know.

Finding himself in front of Ali Baba's house, he tried to commit it to memory. But he found that all the houses in the city resembled one another as one egg does another. So he secretly drew a cross on the door thinking that he would be able to find it again at night. Then he hurried back to his leader to report how cleverly he had contrived everything.

Mardschana, however, was even shrewder than the robber. Although she suspected street urchins when she saw the cross, just to be sure she took a piece of chalk and drew similar crosses on all the houses in the street.

At twilight the robbers set off to attack Ali Baba's house. They hid their sharp sabers and knives under their merchants' clothes and thus disguised went to the city. However, they could not find the house since all the houses in the street bore the same chalk cross and so they had to retreat unsuccessful in their mission. Back in the robber's den they sat in judgment over the spy who had let himself be outwitted like that.

"He must be judged according to our custom," said the leader of the band and the rest of them concurred. So did the robber who was being judged since he knew that he would never be able to continue to live in shame among the robbers. Since it had always been an unwritten robbers' law that whoever failed had to forfeit his life, the robber stood bravely before the leader, who cut off his head with a single blow.

Then Ahmed, the strongest of the group stepped forward, "Brave men! I alone am capable of carrying out such an assignment. And if I don't lead you to the precise spot, then may the same fate befall me." "So be it, Ahmed! If you succeed then all the booty from the house will go to you. If not, then you will lose your head!" answered the robber leader in a serious tone.

Yet things didn't go any better for Ahmed than they had for his predecessor. He did in fact find the right house, cut himself in the finger, and with a drop of blood made a sign in an inconspicuous place next to the door. But this too Mardschana discovered the next day when she was returning from the market where she had just bought some fish. This second sign proved to her that it was no pure coincidence and so she furnished all the houses in the street with the same mark. Only so as not to have to cut her own finger, she simply used the fish's blood.

Yet again the robbers came in vain to the city. Ahmed got shorter by a head and the robber leader fumed with rage.

Even when Kasim, the personal thieving shadow, is no longer alive and Ali Baba sees the danger that this greedy, obsessive, competitive behavior can lead to, the robbers—who more than ever embody these thieving shadows, a collective thieving shadow—are still present. They control the cave with the treasure and if the treasures are to be removed from the cave and integrated into everyday life and if the life-possibilities that one is given are to be ladled out, then these robbers must be conquered.

Initially this battle starts as a contest of wits. Who is more cunning? Who is better able to discern the motives and the intentions of the other party? It becomes clear: Mardschana knows more about getting around robbers than Ali Baba does. She knows what their intentions are. Above all, she is thoroughly familiar with the robbers' evil intentions.

Given that robbers are, among other things, master thieves, it is not surprising that it boils down to a contest of wits.

Hermes, who is the god of the thieves, had the talent of showing people how to become master thieves. He himself is characterized as a master thief because, when he was barely out of his mother's womb, he had already stolen a herd of cattle from his brother Apollo.

Hermes was a god who was always on the move, but he was not only the god of travelers and itinerants. As God's messenger he linked the heaven and the earth, as attendant of the dead, he linked the earth with the underworld. Cunning is a substantial part of his character. Happy discoveries are part of his responsibility. He uncovers things; he also makes many discoveries. He is also responsible for the discoveries that go on at the spiritual level, for interpretation and explanation (hermeneutics). He is also supposed to have invented the dice game and the art of prophecy from the rolling of dice. Thus he is the patron saint of inventors, intellectuals, orators, thieves, merchants.[25] It is his task to ensure that the worlds stay in connection with one another—that the heavens and the earth, the earth and the underworld are linked—so that life undergoes constant transformation and change. The robbers in our story on the other hand, try to hinder this very thing. They try to stop the world from staying in motion and to prevent the exchange from actually taking place. As a result, life stagnates.

Cunning and slyness belong to the robbers; they in turn can be fought only with cunning and slyness. Slyness in the sense of having a good knowledge of life is just what Mardschana possesses.

In fairy tales, cunning is deployed as a method of combat when the situation involves an overwhelming opponent and is a matter of life and death. This also is the scenario here. The question is simply whether the robbers will prevail or Ali Baba, since there do not seem to be any other possibilities and reconciliation is not an option.

The corresponding situation in a human developmental process is difficult to confront. People who find themselves in this situation feel threatened; they withdraw, or they act as though they can ignore the threat. However, they sense that they are in a life situation in which everything is to be decided anew, in which everything can be lost, yet in which everything also can be gained. If the robbers were to win in this fairy tale, then—from a collective point of view—in the conflict with the thieving shadow, nothing would happen. Ali Baba, as the model of a person who has to confront this collective problem, would have failed his fundamental life-task.

Nevertheless, Ali Baba's fear seems to be increasingly held in check, since after all he has delegated the solving of the problem to Mardschana. Mardschana knows the thieving sides; she must already have come into conflict with them.

If a woman lives in a society that is shaped by thieving men, then she learns how to deal with things. Yet also her inner image of man is determined by the thieving behavior. For her it is therefore just as important that she deal with this. If she becomes enslaved by these male thieving sides, then she is likely to lose her female identity. Mardschana seems to have successfully solved this conflict. She stands as a symbol of a woman who is no longer willing to be determined by this thieving shadow, neither in the external world, nor intrapsychically. From this also follows her natural willingness to help. She has learned not to see all men as thieves, but rather to differentiate. In her relationship with Ali Baba she does not behave in a "thieving" way, she does not capitalize on his despair, but instead she stands by him. However, she deals with the robbers consistently, even brutally it seems to us.

In the shorter version of the story, the bravest robber discovers Ali Baba's house very quickly and marks it with a cross. This discovery means that the thieving side is again trying to plague the individual and thus also the more personal Ali Baba. Thus this aspect is re-experienced. It would make sense to be on the alert. The robber has marked the house. Perhaps one could reinterpret the symbol of the cross in its most general meaning of "the integration sign for polar opposites"[26] as heralding the fact that the polar opposites in this story, the robbers and Ali Baba, should be brought together. Naturally the robbers are not going to strive for integration: Ali Baba should die and in this way the problem would be eliminated from the world without the necessity for change. But in the robbers' subconscious choice of the cross as sign, it seems to me that the possibility for some future integration is hinted at. However, this integration of opposites is associated with pain. To begin with, the sign is only a symbol of new developments; advances like this follow one step at a time.

Mardschana shows kindness. She knows about the problem, she is careful. Not particularly worried, she suspects that the street urchins are behind the cross—but she isn't sure. In making a cross on all the houses, she makes the house indistinguishable. Symbolically she simultaneously shows that all people have something of Ali Baba in them and that everyone has to deal with the robber shadow.

That everyone here is alike is also demonstrated by the houses which resemble one another like one egg resembles another. One might also interpret her behavior as meaning that Mardschana suspects that the robber shadow might be active in Ali Baba, yet says nothing about it and even excuses him on account of the fact that all people have light and dark sides in them and simply have to persevere through the tensions that are released.

However, the robbers who wanted to attack Ali Baba's house could not find it. For this the spy loses his life, strictly according to the law of the robbers that dictates that he who fails must forfeit his life. It is a law that allows no weakness.

Incidentally, here the robbers demonstrate another characteristic which might distinguish the robber shadow: there can only be success, since failure means death. Normally life is a tapestry of failure and success. If success alone has a place in life, then we put too many demands on ourselves. Every failure does indeed become a kind of deathly defeat. This state of being can also generate feelings of envy, greed, and desire. In this thieving condition, things very quickly result in defeat, someone else's success implying one's own failure. When one fails, then one tends to feel completely destroyed.

Another robber tries to find Ali Baba. He does not fare any better: he marks the house with blood and to do so, cuts himself on the finger. This second sign assures Mardschana of impending disaster. Again she employs cunning. She administers all the houses with the same sign, using the blood of a fish instead. Thus she does not have to cut her own finger and her cunning does her no harm. Blood, the "sap of life," is regarded as the source of the life force and thus also as the source of the soul. Yet blood also suggests that a problem can become a "bloody" one, that it is a dilemma that could be a matter of life and death. Although the activated robber shadow does not get any further than before, it nonetheless seems to me that it is getting closer—symbolized by this bloody sign. Neither the bravest nor the strongest of the robbers has accomplished the task. As a result, the robber chief, the cleverest of them all, will have to solve the problem himself.

Encountering the Center
of the Shadow

"Tomorrow I will go myself to the city. No one is going to lead me around by the nose. In the meantime, go and find twenty mules and forty big oil jars of which you are to fill only two with oil. And woe be to anyone who gets anything wrong, you bunch of fools!" he added menacingly.

The robbers crept off to their places like whipped dogs and slept fitfully until morning.

It did not occur to the robber leader to make a sign. When he stood in front of Ali Baba's house he simply counted which house it was in the street and before it was even getting dark he was back with his companions.

In the meantime they had carried out all of his orders. Nineteen mules with empty oil jars stood ready and only the twentieth animal carried two full jars.

"Now listen to me carefully!" ordered the leader in a quiet voice. "When we get to just outside the city gate each of you is to climb into a jar. You are not to move until I give you the sign!"

Night fell. In the pale light of the moon the robber leader disguised as a merchant led his caravan of mules through the streets in which Ali Baba lived. He counted the houses and knocked on the right door.

"Who is knocking so late at night?" asked a man's voice from inside and the robber leader answered, "I am a merchant and I have come from afar. I have just arrived in your city and since all the bazaars and inns are closed already, I would like to know if it would not be possible for you to put me and my mules up for the night."

Ali Baba opened the door and saw a strange merchant with tired animals standing in the doorway.

"Greetings, brother, make yourself at home here," he said and led the guest into the inner chamber after telling a servant to take care of the animals.

What more could the robber leader wish? In his wildest dreams it would never have occurred to the unsuspecting Ali Baba that this was his bloodthirsty enemy, the less so when his guest offered him various things that he had supposedly wanted to sell in the city.

They ate, drank, and conversed until late at night when Mardschana wanted to fill the empty oil lamps. But in the whole house there was not a drop of oil to be found. Then it occurred to her that the strange merchant had just offered to sell her master oil. He surely would not mind parting with a few liters for his friends. She took a jug and hurried down to the courtyard. The servant had unloaded the oil jars from the mules and they were now leaning against a wall. Just as Mardschana was about to undo the first jar, a hollow sound emerged from inside, "Is it time yet, captain?"

Anyone else would have fainted in fright, but not Mardschana who right away figured out what was lurking in the plump oil jar. Thinking quickly, she whispered in a disguised voice, "Not yet. Wait a moment!"

Then she went from jar to jar. At each of them she repeated the same trick until she came to the end of the row and had counted thirty-eight robbers.

Only in the last two jars did she really find oil and this gave her an idea. She carried a large cauldron from the kitchen, poured in oil from the jars, and lit a fire under the cauldron. Then she fanned the fire until the oil began to boil and poured the bubbling oil into the jars directly onto the heads of the robbers. The bandits who had long held the area in fear and terror died miserable deaths.

The robber chief is the ringleader of the robbers. From a symbolic point of view, embodied in him is everything associated with thievery. It is he who dictates the relationship with the world. When we speak about a thieving shadow that is based in a thieving complex, then it is this shadow which is expressed in the robber chief. We have to assume contact with him if we are to work through the shadow realm. Otherwise he will make contact with us whenever the shadow realm in our spiritual economy requires a lot of energy and tries to take over the ego, and when we find ourselves in danger and continually behaving like thieves.

If Kasim can be seen as Ali Baba's personal shadow, then the robber chief can be regarded as the representative of the collective shadow. By this is meant, that a whole epoch can come under the sway of a thieving shadow. The conflict with the shadow can be accomplished by people whose personal shadow has been infected with it. However, that such a thing as a collective shadow actually exists gives rise to the fact that our own personal outlook is always being externally influenced, and that we often feel like "hangers-on" to other people who have the same mind-set. This fairy story clearly expresses the idea that the collective shadow that each and every one of us respectively participate in holds the treasure within its power. It is for this reason that the shadow must be combatted.

Twenty mules have to be procured and forty oil jars. Previously the robbers rode horses. Ali and his brother normally used donkeys, the usual beast of burden. The mule is a cross between a horse and a donkey. The choice of animal by the robbers shows they have somewhat come down off their high horse, that the cross between horse and donkey has already taken place. And that cross is symbolic of the linking of opposites between Ali Baba and the robbers.

So what cunning does the robber himself employ? He disguises himself as an oil dealer bringing oil so that lamps can burn, so that there can be more light. Yet what on the one hand is simply profane light can also be seen on a symbolic level as illumination, as being seized by a holy light. In Sufi mysticism light plays an important role since "God is of course also light."[27] Lamps made of clay that burn oil are often regarded as representing human beings, who are also symbolically made of earth and whose life flame can either burn or go out. Thus oil is seen as synonymous with the life force. The light symbolism connects oil, which comes from plants,to the sky, the realm of the sun. The connection between earth and sky that we found in the symbolism of the tree is again emphasized—and this is what this fairy story is ultimately about: that the earth gets what it deserves and so does the sky; that women aren't slaves and men aren't robbers; that women and men do not have to outwit one another, but rather should use cunning to overcome common dangers—and should love one another.

So the robber chief poses as a merchant who functions in the service of light. However, we know that he is carrying with him thirty-eight jars containing the robbers and only two containing oil. As yet nothing much has changed in the realm of the robber complex. But the robber chief wants to outwit us by transforming that which he embodies into its diametrical opposite.

The robber chief comes late at night, during the time when we are more at the mercy of our dark sides since we have them less well under control, when feelings of fear can be triggered more easily. When dawn comes, we once more deem those things which had so terrified us during the night considerably less frightening in the light of day.

For this very reason, the robber chief comes by night.

Ali Baba welcomes him unsuspectingly—most likely a gesture of hospitality, but also typical for him, his naiveté, his lack of awareness about the shadow realm.

If we look at the scene from a symbolic perspective, then in passing we might point out that Ali Baba is now standing opposite his thieving shadow without being aware of the fact. The shadow has found entry into his house, and now comes the decisive confrontation. But Ali Baba doesn't know that he is engaged in conversation with the robber chief. We too are frequently unaware that we are already conversing with our thieving shadow, particularly on occasions like this one when it appears in disguise. As long as our shadow sides do not wear a mask and appear to be what they are, then we are able to recognize them. But who in the world would suspect that behind a merchant who seems to be travel-weary, there is really a robber in disguise?

Yet it is the very mask itself that shows us which camouflage our most important shadow sides reveal. Not infrequently the shadow appears to us as its polar opposite, the thieving shadow acts particularly modestly. In this lies not only confusion, but also, of course, a deeper meaning: Through its opposite which we also experience, the shadow is relativized and can be better accepted. Through this process of dealing with the opposite, we can confront the shadow much more easily.

In Ali Baba's case, it is to be assumed that his thieving shadow has found admittance into his dealings as a merchant. Presumably he is also a little too mercenary when it comes to making a profit. The collective thieving shadow seems harmless, "businesslike," in the sense of: I'm entitled to it, I need it after all, there's no harm in it . . .

Ali Baba is depicted as being guileless: he has obviously largely lost his fear of the robbers, probably in part because he has delegated the solving of the problem to Mardschana. When we experience an element of the shadow realm that threatens our psyche, then we have to be ever on guard against ourselves, just like Mardschana is. Otherwise there exists the danger that we will act from the perspective of the shadow realm and not with the responsibility of the "I." Ali Baba however has become unsuspecting—and when we are unsuspecting, then we are no longer vigilant.

By this late hour the lamps have burnt low and they need to be replenished with oil. The illumination is weaker: wakefulness is ebbing. Darkness could descend. If we interpret the light of the lamps as the life-light, then we see that life itself is threatened, or life as it has been hitherto lived.

The slave—and this is probably also her job—is awake and wants to refill the oil lamps, but there is no more oil in the house. A strange confluence of events: in such a wealthy household with such a prudent slave, the oil has run out. One has to draw the conclusion that the oil *had* to run out. One could also make the link here with the interpretation of the New Testament parable about the clever girl and the foolish girl—in the sense that in this fairy story there is also a tremendous pervading hopelessness—as with the foolish girl whose oil ran out.

It is also possible that the fairy story wants to convey the idea that new oil is now called for, that there is a need for another life force, a new force, a new substance from which something new can shine. However, this also means that a fundamental transformation is necessary and that now these shadow sides have to be dealt with in a decidedly different manner than before.

In any case, the lack of oil brings about contact between Mardschana and the robbers. Symbolically, it refers again to the robbers as those who are at the root of the problem.

The robbers in the oil jars—a covering which is reminiscent of intrauterine life—are now concealed in a cave that is considerably less comfortable that their robbers' den. Just as it was the robber chief's cunning that led him to have his robbers appear as "oil," now it is Mardschana's cunning that allows her to pass herself off as the robber chief and to redeploy the oil to mercilessly destroy the robbers. Here it is once again clear why she is able to so successfully confront these robber sides: She knows them well—if necessary she can also pass as a robber chief without actually being one.

She boils the oil in a cauldron—and pours the hot oil into the jars. The cauldron, a vessel that in contradistinction to the oil jar has a large opening, is the place where food can be transformed into something enjoyable or something made more enjoyable. Symbolically, this also alludes to the capacity to transform people and the fact that in the final analysis everything can—and indeed must—be transformed. Also the woman's womb is regarded as a vessel for the developing human being.[28] For this reason, the cauldron was originally always in the possession of a priestess or a witch. She mixed the potions that could save life or bring death. The hearth fire is also a more female kind of fire, which has metamorphosis as its goal—unlike light, the purpose of which is illumination.

Hot oil burns, scorches. Through fire the oil, which itself can be a fuel for fire, becomes hot, deadly hot. The fire metaphors in this story also represent inner fire. The story has to do with a passionate fire of love for life, as well as a passionate rage against thievery which ultimately causes these thieving sides to be eliminated, to prevail no longer, and henceforth to cease to be a threat. Here in the end it becomes clear that Mardschana is confronting these thieving sides as though they were her own sides, which in fact they are. Using the means that the robber chief has himself placed in her hands, she fights the robbers. This is a legitimate course of action that we can experience in our conflict with our shadows in our everyday lives : Our shadow sides also correspond to particular positions and ways of behaving. So long as our shadow is threatened, we suppress the fact that we possess such behavior patterns. Our fellow human beings are well aware of the fact, but we ourselves don't want to admit to the fact. But it is just the very behavior patterns that do not correspond to our ideal ways of behaving that are very useful for dealing with the shadow sides. With our thieving sides we quickly grasp what advantage promises, we seize opportunities before others have a chance to take them away from us. It is this very characteristic that we can employ in order to discover the thieving side in ourselves and to consciously let it become visible.

Among other things, the thieving side expresses itself through brutality. If as in this instance, it's a case of life being threatened by the thieving side, then in turn one has to use force to deal with it. Were one less threatened, one might perhaps be able to negotiate, to be milder.

Dancing, Unmasking the Shadow

Having thus rendered the robbers harmless, she went back into the house as though nothing had happened. She filled up the lamps, put on her dancing outfit, and accompanied by the servant Abdallah, who held a drum in his hand, re-entered the hall.

Ali Baba was impressed by her and said to his guest, "Sir, this woman is really a treasure. She is not only an outstanding servant, but also the most charming dancer I have ever seen. And besides, she is extraordinarily clever; who else would have come up with the delightful idea of increasing our pleasure with the sight of her dancing?"

The robber leader just nodded, cleverly hiding his rage and impatience. He longed for the moment when he could exact his revenge—and now he would have to wait even longer!

Abdallah beat the drum and Mardschana swayed to the dance. She moved so gently and gracefully, her feet barely touching the floor, and her youthful countenance beamed like a newly blossoming flower in the spring.

The dance came to an end. The young woman took the drum from Abdallah's hand and bowed before Ali Baba, receiving a reward from him. She got her dinar and then stepped up to the false merchant with the same act. The robber leader also tried to take a dinar out of his breast pocket, but in so doing accidentally revealed the dagger that he kept concealed and ready.

At that moment Mardschana grabbed the dagger and stabbed the villain in the heart so that right then and there he breathed his last and exhaled his evil soul.

"You unfortunate one! What have you done?" shouted Ali Baba angrily. "You won't escape punishment!" "Calm down, my lord," responded Mardschana calmly. "This man was no foreign merchant, but rather the head of the terrible robber band who wanted to do you in. Come with me and see the proof for yourself!"

And she led him to the courtyard and the oil jars. To Ali Baba's horror there was no oil in the jars but instead thirty-eight dead robbers. And then she told him about how she had found the signs and had twice deceived the robbers.

At this point in the longer version there is another scene depicted which is missing from our version: In this scene, instead of waiting up with the robber chief, Ali Baba goes to bed. The robber chief then throws pebbles at the oil jars when he is sure that no one is still awake; this is the predetermined signal upon which the robbers are supposed to open the jars and emerge. When no one reacts to the pebbles "fear crept in his heart."[29] He starts to look, but already from the first oil jar the smell of burned oil wafts toward him. He goes along from jar to jar and tries to speak to the robbers. But "they maintained their icy silence. . . . A wild grief came over him and he cried bitterly over the loss of his comrades".[30] Fearing capture himself, he flees. Mardschana however, has observed everything and closes the garden gate behind him.

Later we learn that, upon returning to the treasure trove, the robber chief weeps because he feels so abandoned. "He fell to the ground in pain, grieving that he had only been bestowed with disappointment and that his deeds had all worked against him. He longed for his people and had no desire to live; indeed he longed for death."[31]

Finally he swears revenge. He wants to wipe out the disgrace. He sets himself up as a merchant in the bazaar occupying the shop opposite that of Mohammed, Ali Baba's young son. He knows how to become his friend and thus how to gain entry into Ali Baba's home.

The shorter version of the story skips this part, in which it once again becomes clear to what extent the desire for revenge plays in thievish behavior and how any means of deception can be justified when it comes to achieving the goal of revenge. Here, too, it is clear how relationships are exploited in order to carry out plans for revenge and how the values of a relationship are transgressed in a thievish manner.

In reading the description of the grieving robber, we almost feel a little pity for the robber chief who is suffering so much from this loss. It almost seems as though he possesses an iota of human sentiment; at this moment his comrades are more than just instruments of power. Yet it is this very thing which emerges as a danger in our interaction with our shadow sides: Suddenly we find that they aren't so bad. Almost coquettishly, we coddle the last remnants of troublesome behavior patterns from the past. If, however, the shadow is as dangerous as this thieving shadow, then such coddling comes at a high price.

It is a sense of loss that the robber chief brings to his wicked plans for revenge. This is the reason why I have included the section so comprehensively. And of course one finds in turn a clear parallel with the framing story: The sultan Scheherban tries to kill all women because one of them has been unfaithful to him: a thieving attitude tolerates no separation, no failure; it cannot deal with loss. Accepting loss is the preserve of others. Thievish behavior responds to loss with revenge, seeks out the perpetrators and haunts them. Aside from this, it becomes clear that a thieving attitude cannot tolerate bonds and loss, but rather only bonds. Loss is threatening. Separations are a great affliction that are supposed to be dealt with by all sorts of machinations and thoughts of revenge.

In the abbreviated version of the story, Mardschana having killed the robbers, puts on her dancing outfit and performs for Ali Baba and the robber chief—to Ali Baba's delight and the guest's displeasure. This gives Ali Baba the opportunity to praise the virtues of the slave: she is an excellent servant, a pearl, extraordinarily clever, and the most charming dancer. Charm, beauty, reliability, and intelligence are all combined in this one person. With the killing of the robbers, she demonstrates that she is also extraordinarily courageous and moreover is very determined. While dancing she shows an entirely other side of herself, that of exhilaration; she thus comes across as the very embodiment of femininity.

Even if Ali Baba sees this dance as a means of intensifying pleasure, and even if this is customary in the Orient after a good meal, the dance still embodies a deeper meaning. The dance puts the human being's body and soul into motion. One feels unusually airy and light. Dancing one feels thoroughly moved, transported, seized by a life-feeling that comes over one. This life-feeling can be intensified to the point of ecstasy.

With this dance Mardschana expresses the sense of wholeness. Standing there on the floor she shows the lightness of her being and is all the while completely herself, moving to a rhythm that is entirely her own. In so doing, she shows great "natural emotion" and she conveys this emotion to Ali Baba. There is nothing thievish in this, merely the pleasure of being alive, a feeling of delight in the self—of knowing that the earth and the sky belong to one. This is beauty—which is also an experience of wholeness, the sense of being at one with the self.

While dancing, the mode of having has nothing to search for. We are simply in the mode of being, totally dedicated to the experience and the moment. The thieving shadow would have to compare who is dancing more beautifully, would have to signal whether or not one should feel envious. Were this the case, however, then one would no longer be a dancer but at best just someone in motion.

What this example of the dance demonstrates is something that is valid as a life-lesson in general. Life too can be a dance—at least from time to time—and we lose this sense of mobile emotion when our thieving shadow emphasizes having too much.

On the other hand, we cannot totally get away from having things: Mardschana wants a reward for her dance and so she receives a dinar from Ali Baba and a dagger from the robber chief, the dagger with which she can ultimately stab him.

It is only with the experience of wholeness expressed in the dance—expressed directly by Mardschana and in loving contemplation by Ali Baba—that the thieving shadow can completely disappear and is forced to breathe its last. Only when the combination of eroticism, beauty, and emotion is tangible does the thieving shadow become superfluous.

On Ali Baba's part, during the course of Mardschana's dance he becomes aware of what qualities this slave possesses, and of the fact that she can also convey values that are not just associated with having.

For the most part I have referred to Mardschana in terms of her relationship with Ali Baba, as someone who has in a downright motherly fashion even alleviated his problems for him. However, at the end of this scene it becomes clear that she also presents an image of her own unconscious-spiritual femininity. In Ali Baba's fascination with her dance, her charm, and her intelligence, what he seems to admire most is her spiritual mobility expressed through these aspects of her life. This mobility is conveyed to him by her, and as a result these values are also brought to life in his psyche, releasing in him a feeling of completeness, of amazement, and of love. Through Mardschana, the treasure in the cave finally becomes accessible to him. Spiritual–erotic liveliness does not have to hoard anything: the robber chief can make his exit. Yet Ali Baba still does not suspect the connection, and he is immediately prepared to see evil in Mardschana's undertakings! But he quickly sees reason when Mardschana is able to reveal the true state of affairs. Ali Baba is able to listen.

Liberating Female Intelligence:
Or, the Opened-up Treasure

Ali Baba could not praise Mardschana's cleverness enough. As a token of his thankfulness he released her from slavery and married her to his son, since he had long been aware that the two young people were not indifferent to one another. And a cleverer and truer daughter-in-law he could hardly have hoped for.

However there was one thing that Mardschana could not account for: what had happened to the two missing robbers. At the time, Ali Baba had counted forty robbers apart from the leader outside the cave, but there were only thirty-eight in the oil jars. What she could not know was that the robber leader had disposed of these two with his own hands.

Thus for an entire year Ali Baba did not venture into the cave and only when he had persuaded himself that no one had been there the whole time was he able to get some peace.

Until the end of his days he lived in peace and prosperity, fetching from the robbers' den only as much as he needed. And all his life Mardschana was the only person who knew the secret, since Ali Baba had learned only too well what envy and greed could do.[32]

Mardschana becomes a free woman: she is released from slavery and is wed to Mohammed, Ali Baba's own son. Ali Baba knew that the two young people fancied one another. They are in fact married by the father, but he does so with their approval. There is love between them.

Ali Baba is thankful to the slave and he shows his gratitude—she need not be a slave any longer—and at the same time, he is sure that there isn't a cleverer and truer daughter-in-law anywhere. He trusts in the fidelity of a woman who can give freely, without any strings attached, and he also recognizes her intelligence.

If we turn to the framing story again, then it becomes apparent the extent to which the position of women has changed. In the framing story, the women were in actual fact all slaves. Now however, in Mardschana we have a free woman, for like Scheherezade, Mardschana is set free.

In the framing story, cunning is instigated by women in an effort to protect themselves against the shackles imposed on them by men. In this tale, cunning is deployed as a way of combatting the thievery manifest in the behavior of men. In this manner, there is a clear distinction made between Ali Baba and the robbers. At the same time, Mardschana's cunning more closely resembles the wisdom of Scheherezade.

To be sure Mardschana is very well acquainted with the robbers' foibles. In her conclusive struggle with the robbers, she simultaneously fights against what is thievish in her own soul and thereby also frees Ali Baba from the danger imposed by the robbers. Whenever a given time period is so dominated by thievery, then naturally men and women are affected. However, Mardschana never was really in danger of being overpowered by the robbers .

In this fairy story and in the framing story, it becomes clear that the relationship between men and women is determined by the thieving impulse, that women very easily can become the slaves of thieving men. At a symbolic level, this can also be seen as the attempt on the part of the masculine to keep the feminine under control. Underlying this urge is the fantasy of wanting and being able to have everything—of erecting a paradise, a land of Cockaigne in a cave.

However if we intend only to possess this treasure, then life does not actually show its immeasurable wealth. Instead we get a glimpse of the harsh rejection, symbolized by the rock.

The story "Ali Baba and the Forty Thieves" shows a state of affairs between man and woman as it is expressed in the framing story and its consequences: Ali Baba is already very poor; the treasure cave filled with beauty, with a wealth of sensual pleasures which delight people, excite them, and stimulate them, is in the hands of the robbers. By encountering the robbers, Ali Baba becomes aware of his thieving side. Because he admits his fear of the robbers and calls on Mardschana for help, the situation ultimately improves to the extent that entry into the cave is guaranteed—an essential aspect of life has in turn become accessible to everyday life. For her part, Mardschana provides not only her unselfish assistance, but also her considered intelligence. Over and over again it is stressed how intelligent Mardschana is. In this, as well as in her helpful demeanor and the way in which she considers everyone's best interests, she resembles Scheherezade, who tells the sultan stories so that he will finally stop killing young women.

Above all, Mardschana's intelligence consists in the fact that she uses cunning as a way of overcoming whatever is disruptive. From the beginning Ali Baba is aware of the intelligence of women and he entrusts himself to this intelligence when he no longer knows where to turn. In this regard he is much further developed than the Sultan Scheherban. We may assume that in Ali Baba's personal make-up there is personified a developmental level that corresponds to Scheherban and that this level was made possible through the telling of stories.

However, Ali Baba and Mardschana are still on guard against the robbers. They cannot after all be sure that all forty really are dead. And it probably is better so: when thieving sides are fought, whether one at a time in life or collectively, then we always need to count on the fact that some of these sides will reappear. Generally it's not as easy as it is in this story to solve the problem once and for all.

Entry to the cave is now possible, and from the cave we can take whatever is needed and whatever is pleasing.

The abbreviated version of the story differs from the longer version to the extent that Mardschana alone shares the secret. In the other version Ali Baba goes to the cave with his son Mohammed, who is likewise completely amazed. The short version is also more moralistic when it comes to envy and greed. It shows Ali Baba as a person who, despite his great wealth, does not want to provoke envy or solicit greed in others. In the other version, Ali Baba and Mohammed only take what they have always longed for from the cave and live a wonderful and happy life until they die.

Even if the longer version ends rather paradisiacally, it expresses more the joy over the discovery of the great treasure. This joy seems very significant to me, and leaving it out just to underline the theme of envy seems to me yet another devaluation of what has been achieved.

It also doesn't make sense that the treasure should be hoarded, particularly since this treasure is seen as a collection of things that convey Eros and pleasure for the senses, a glimpse of which might provide us with an idea of the absolute beauty that in Islamic mysticism is an expression of the deity. If this is so, then these beautiful things should be transmitted to everyone so that all of us might be able to experience the richness. In the life of a Sufi mystic, it was essential to pass things on by conveying what was seen to one's pupils.

If a mystical element really is linked to this experience of the cave, and Ali Baba is also really a "Baba," then he must convey to people what he has learned here, namely how to deal with the thieving shadow. Incidentally, this thieving shadow often plays a very large role in such cultures because they are founded on a mystical–ascetic tradition (like Christianity) which restricts the natural impulse to seize life and take pleasure in one's riches. The shadow represents whatever it is that we are incapable of reconciling with our ego-ideal or else with a collective ideal. For this reason we always have to deal with shadows, since every ideal in turn creates a shadow. And this is also why the conflict with the shadow is a never-ending task.

In this story the thieving shadow leads to the principle of having, to greed and envy; rivalry in relationships with people of the same sex; dominating, exploitative relationships with the opposite sex, and also with the riches of the earth. We will only be able to dispense with the thieving shadow when men are able to consult their street-smart, courageous female sides, as represented by Mardschana, and recognize them for their full worth, and women on the other hand are able to confront the thieving shadow and make the distinction between men and "robbers." Then instead of mutual domination, it may be possible to cultivate real relationships into which the participants feel free to bring their treasures.

If the *anima* is accepted in this way, then Mardschana can marry Mohammed, the son of Ali Baba, as a free woman. The pair of them, Mardschana and Mohammed, both externally and internally, belong to the future.

As an inner couple, Mardschana would represent a masculine side that had nothing thievish about it, and Mohammed would represent a clever emotive and relational feminine side. The struggle between the sexes could thus be abandoned, at least for the time being.

Analogous with the pair Mardschana–Mohammed is the pair Scheherzade–Scheherban at the end of the collection of fairy stories of *A Thousand and One Nights*. The story of "Ali Baba and the Forty Thieves" is a story en route to Scheherban's learning how to be capable of a relationship, whereas previously he had felt compelled to kill women. It is a story which shows that the thieving shadow must be confronted and how one might go about doing so, if one really wants to attain the ability to have a relationship.

Aside from this, the fairy story also shows that accepting the life-wisdom of women is an important aspect in accepting a new image of women. Scheherezade, the wise woman, shows an aspect of herself in Mardschana, with her pragmatic, clever nature—which is certainly a part of wisdom. Aside from cleverness and wisdom, these women also possess unalterable courage: they make no reproaches; they simply do what has to be done in the service of life.

This story which apparently deals with an old problem actually seems to me to be of great contemporary relevance. It is, after all, our relationship with Mother Nature that is characterized by thievery. And many of our relationships fall under the law of domination and subjugation, in which the subjugated can easily become masters again.

It seems to me that having a feel for the riches of life and an awe about them are sentiments that get lost too easily, perhaps because we believe that we are entitled to everything anyway and perhaps even more.

A debate with the thieving shadow is certainly due—for women as well as for men.

SISYPHVS

The Old Stone—The New Way

A Labor of Sisyphus

One day as I was yet again clearing away a mountain of dishes, it occurred to me just how soon the next mountain of dishes would appear—and I suddenly became aware of how many more mountains of dishes would follow that one, not to mention how many I had already washed. It is work that in uniform regularity repeats itself over and over again and is only temporarily finished: work that will always be repeated—a real labor of Sisyphus, this eternal clearing away of dishes.

Once I had put a name to it, it occurred to me that as long as I can remember, the news on the radio has all seemed the same: always the same old problems in the world being discussed and debated without anything really changing. At the same time, we always hear the kind of reporting that attaches great significance to unhappiness in the world and very little importance to happy things.

I saw a connection between my endless, repetitive work and the perpetually recurring problems of humanity, which likewise never seem to get resolved. Naturally I might have directed my attention instead to the sense of satisfaction which accompanies the moment when the mountain of dishes has been cleared away, or to the little advances which one can similarly see in the "news" of human progress. But on this day what struck me was the aspect of eternal repetition, accompanied by the certainty that so much in life is about starting over, right at the very point when a big change would really be nice.

Other experiences related to this issue came to mind. I thought for example, of the number of times I have tried to explain the same subject, or the number of times I have approached a problem from all possible angles, thinking that I have solved it, only to find that I have not understood it well enough or formulated it concisely enough. I have to formulate it again, reformulate it—and here, too, start all over again.

Although I was quite certain that clearing away dishes undoubtedly constituted a "labor of Sisyphus," I was less certain of this when it came to the issue of human beings' struggling with their problems as expressed on the news. I was even more unsure when I tried to come up with explanations. Questions that we ask over and over may resemble one another closely, but the situations that generate them frequently differ or change somehow. The struggle for a concise expression or an appropriate image may well seem like eternal repetition, as do the components of some prior success. I don't really characterize this work as a labor of Sisyphus. Even though there is a lot that is Sisyphean about it, there is too much change associated with it to identify it that way.

Then I thought about people undergoing therapy who struggle continually with the same basic problems. They always ask the same questions and have the same characteristics which lead to conflict. Many of them complain, "Won't I ever get a grip on this problem?," and feel almost driven to distraction by their efforts. Later, they are able to see things from a different vantage point, and even though they are dealing with the same problems, realize that they are now able to deal with them differently. Although the first time around they are completely convinced that the work in and of itself—the fundamental problem—is a labor of Sisyphus, the next time around they are slightly less adamant about it.

Naturally the question arises as to whether a labor of Sisyphus becomes less of an effort if we succeed in being able to see not only the repetition, but also the very subtle change that is occurring. Or is it just that we call something a labor of Sisyphus when we are unable or unwilling to see a change?

Clearly it is hard to see meaning in a labor of Sisyphus that really is merely repetitive, for we associate meaning with transformation and conclusion.

Pushing the Stone

The Second Part of the Myth of Sisyphus

My everyday experience washing dishes was a pretext for combining an underlying feeling I had with a mythical image. My resistance to eternal repetition was placed in a larger context through the connection with a mythological image and the existential experience of people who must continually struggle in vain.

Myths are stories that are constructed out of elements of everyday experiential reality. In addition, we use these connections to express our own self-understanding, our experience of the deity, and our position relative to both the deity and to the real world. If a myth is to endure, then it must express not only a collective but also an individual reality, and it must express a fundamental existential experience or longing.

Because much of myth has been demythologized by historiography, myths only really reveal their symbolic function when they are alive—in other words, when they still speak to us. Myths refer to basic existential experiences. Every myth articulates some special core fear or hope. When we deal with myths, then we are dealing with basic existential experiences. In the myth of Sisyphus, for example, we are dealing with the experience of a person who, at least on the surface, struggles in vain but cannot bring himself to abandon the task. I say "on the surface" because the phrase already implies a deeper meaning to the myth.

Sisyphus is supposed to be "successful": he is supposed to roll the stone up and over the hill in order to complete his task. Is he really supposed to do so? Don't we often characterize a task as a labor of Sisyphus and our efforts as Sisyphean simply because we are totally convinced that a goal must be reached and reached as quickly as possible?

Homer's Odysseus recalls seeing Sisyphus on his journey through the Underworld:

> Yes, I also got a glimpse of Sisyphus,
> who slaved away in suffering;
> he pushed a huge block
> with both hands.
> In truth, he pushed it up to the top
> and leaned against it,
> using his feet and hands; yet it was so far up
> that the height
> finally got the better of him and the load pushed
> him backwards.
> Then the shameless stone rolled down the hill again.
> But again he started to slave away and pushed
> so that his body was dripping with sweat
> and around his head there was a cloud of dust.[1]

This part of the myth is well-known. It conveys the experience of great exertion, intense effort, and staying-power even though the intended goal is not attained. From this follows the eternal repetition—which in the myth is a punishment doled out by the gods.

The myth of Sisyphus, like all myths that are germane, expresses a fundamental human experience, an aspect of our very life and being.

Everyday Interpretations
of the Myth

That this myth is still germane, that it still touches and effects people, was evident from the reaction of my peers when I told them I was currently working on the Sisyphus myth. A sigh, a laugh, a look of understanding, sometimes bitter, sometimes bittersweet—everyone let me know that this problem was not unknown to them. The result was several conversations about resignation, the need to persevere, the meaning and absurdity of existence. People expressed feelings of being overextended, of being unable to support this rock any longer and of simply not wanting to continue to do so. They posed questions that conjured up a sense of both hope and hopelessness. Depending on the life situation in which the individuals found themselves, there were different aspects of this rich mythical image that were emphasized: Some people experienced it primarily as a laborious and heavy stone that they had to prop up, as the symbol of an eternal task that was a kind of torture to them. For others, the eternal repetition itself was the torturous thing: the eternal repetition was what made the "stone" heavy to them. And in fact most of them agreed that in the end it was both the burden and the repetition that were so difficult.

But there were other reactions as well. There were some people who experienced the repetition as beneficial, as an expression of a kind of order that one could depend upon. They felt at one with themselves doing the same thing over and over. To them this expressed the very nature of life. If one person missed a sense of discovery in this way of life, others were perfectly comfortable with the fact that innovation wasn't in the foreground.

These different reactions to the myth very quickly told me that the myth can be experienced in different ways, but also that the reactions are contingent upon the role that the myth plays in the respective life situations of individual people. After all, it is probably clear that the myth of Sisyphus does not express every aspect of human existence. There are many myths that articulate other essential aspects of human existence and which respectively illuminate different perspectives. For example, in contradistinction to the Sisyphus myth, there are myths about the divine child, which deal with the creative power and inventiveness of human beings. The myth of Sisyphus can never be a model for all human existence as a whole. Nonetheless, it is noteworthy that this mythological motif is well-known to so many people, probably because our language uses the idiom "a labor of Sisyphus." And depending on how old we are, there are certain aspects of this myth that come to the fore and others that recede into the background.

Associations

*"What do you think of when you hear the term,
'a labor of Sisyphus'?"*

A nineteen-year-old woman: "A labor of Sisyphus? Useless work, work that isn't any good to anyone. Just frustration. You should avoid it whenever possible."

A twenty-two-year-old man: "A labor of Sisyphus? Work that is done for no purpose and that is also difficult. It is something that is probably part of all work processes. I think that a labor of Sisyphus is only justified when the whole work process produces something worthwhile, when something new comes out of it."

A forty-year-old woman: "A labor of Sisyphus! I don't really see it as being useless. I see more the eternal repetition. Take housework for example, the washing—it's always the same old thing. But of course it's all necessary. Or what about when you always have the same problems in your relationship and you try over and over again to solve them, but it's always unproductive. Sometimes I just want to do everything completely differently."

A forty-two-year-old man: "That guy who was always rolling that stone—that's how I think of myself. Lots of things that used to be a challenge just aren't challenging anymore. The effort is still there, but I don't get that feeling of triumph any-more—only the hard work. Actually the challenge is probably in just being able to put up with the lack of challenge. But I am already pretty much resigned to things. There's not that much energy left over for other things. Besides which, for most people it's normal to have to carry this load. In the past I was admired; now normally, at the most I get criticized."

A seventy-five-year-old woman: "A labor of Sisyphus. I haven't thought about it in a long time. In the past, when I was between forty and fifty or so, there was so much to do and there was always something new. It seemed as though there was no end in sight. When I think about the mountains of socks that I always had to mend—and they always got holes in them again. I thought it was pointless. I often cried with rage. The work has diminished now, at least the external work. One day I simply must have accepted everything. Of course, there is always another side to things: when everything just gets dirty again, then one doesn't really need to clean as if one were cleaning for all eternity. Things are just the way they are; everything repeats itself. And there is something beautiful about that. It also gives you a feeling of being familiar with life. You develop strategies for dealing with things, begin to do things a little differently. And at some point, I guess I just felt proud of myself. These days I see the problem as being much more an internal one. I have qualities that have always made life hard for me—and that still do. I probably consciously have dealt with them for thirty years already: there's always this eternal father-complex thing. Of course, I also know that it can't really be any other way. But I still don't give up fighting."

A seventy-three-year-old man: "I was a teacher. I still won-der today where I got the strength to teach students the same thing over and over again. There were always the same problems, the same questions. Sometimes I thought it was real a labor of Sisyphus when I got discouraged and had the feeling that students just didn't learn what was important. But of course that's not really the case. I only thought about Sisyphus when I was discouraged or when I wanted too much. Now I'm thinking about Sisyphus in connection with death. In this way, throughout my whole life, I have put my back to this stone. I haven't run away. You could always leave the stone lying there and just take off. And now I'm actually not that sure whether doing what I did was the right thing or not."

When we compare these responses with one another, it becomes clear that everyone talked about Sisyphus in connection with work. In other words, the myth of Sisyphus is one that we associate with working people. Perhaps it really is a myth about work. This idea is reinforced when we consider the fact that we use the expression "a labor of Sisyphus"—which is also one of the ways of interpreting the myth. In comparison with this, the Sisyphus theme is one that emerges above all during mid-life. This is when it is clearly experienced at an existential level. It is no longer so easy as it was at a younger age to dispense with the problems that arise. Younger people certainly encounter the problem of a labor of Sisyphus and feel frustration, but then it is a frustration that is avoidable. With middle-aged people, it seems as though a labor of Sisyphus is no longer so easy to avoid. It is more often regarded as "necessary," and in fact it is this very condition of necessity that links it to unproductiveness. Something that is necessary doesn't have to be unproductive, but necessary repetition often prompts us to ask whether or not the task has any meaning. It is clear that we fear that the things we think are necessary might perhaps in the long-run turn out to be futile. Perhaps what is also at stake is the tension between knowing that not everything can be productive, and an internalized demand that everything must be productive. The necessity of repetition seems to be accepted, and yet it stands in contradiction to our demand that life must change. This is the tension that is embodied by the myth of Sisyphus. It is a dilemma that causes us to consider whether the repetition is really necessary or whether it is simply an attempt to solve something in an unproductive way.

The forty-year-old woman speaks of a labor of Sisyphus in connection with relationships. Here it is no longer just external work that is seen as repetition, but also our behavior within relationships. The same "peculiarities" that change so little always result in the same behavior, the same complaints we have about one another result in the kind of argument that never gets anywhere because both parties already know the outcome—it is "the same old record" playing over and over—and no one is capable of making the slightest little change.

"Unproductive" is probably an apt description of this state of affairs because we know so well exactly how it is that our partner should be. It is also unproductive because we have grown accustomed to these repetitions. Perhaps we have had several relationships like this and this state of affairs is no longer cause for alarm, nor is it a wake-up call.

Finally the question arises as to whether or not it is reasonable to perservere at a problem—Sisyphus is after all just one myth amongst many. In many instances, this perseverance might well be just meaningless repetition.

The forty-two-year-old man experiences an altogether different aspect of this myth. His associations make clear why the Sisyphus myth might perhaps be deemed the myth of the forty-year-old.

Lots of things that have to do with mastering life—at least externally—are things that are learned and applied. Strangely enough, that great feeling we get when we first achieve something we thought was beyond our capabilities is unrepeatable. At best, we can remember what it was like. For the most part however, achievement becomes "commonplace." We have gotten used to it and so have the people around us. But we have a hard time adjusting to this sense of being "commonplace"—perhaps also because we have put all our energy into our work and have no energy left for anything else. We have here a forty-year-old for whom this myth explains a lot; does this mean that his life is dictated by the Sisyphean? Has he perhaps learned that by really shouldering the stone he will reach the summit?

It becomes increasingly clear how important it is for us to accord the theme of the Sisyphean a specific place in our lives.

Aside from this, what becomes clear is a phenomenon that only indirectly has something to do with the myth of Sisyphus, but which can considerably intensify our suffering from the Sisyphus dilemma: admiration is something that we are accorded more often as youths and young adults than we are later in life. In later life there is a lot that repeats itself; lots of things become "commonplace," even expected. People who do not have a sense of self-worth unless they have accomplished something truly spectacular and are troubled by the commonplace find the Sisyphean more torturous than it already is.

My hunch that the Sisyphus dilemma is the preserve of forty-somethings is supported by the assertions of the seventy-five-year-old woman. In her case feelings of meaninglessness arose when it came to the endless socks that had to be darned. She felt angry about doing a job that could never be completed. And then she simply accepted everything as being one aspect of ordinary life as opposed to "eternal life"—the fact that some human endeavors are never finished. She found meaning in human limitations: the struggle was no longer worthless simply because it didn't result in something absolute. The eternal repetition is accepted. Out of this eternal repetition comes a certain "familiarity" with life. For example, we repeat certain things so that we remember them. In repeating them, we learn to face life as it is, if we aren't continually confronted by new, unforeseeable situations.

Based on the story this woman tells, it is also very clear that we can outgrow a phase of life in which the Sisyphus theme dominates: at first she suffered from it, even rebelled, and then accepted it as a possible fact of life. By virtue of this fact, her striving for the absolute became relative and the positive aspects of repetition—the feeling of security in repetition—could be experienced. However, she then points out the ways in which she makes up for her need for change, something that is peculiar to every life: The tasks may have been the same ones, but she always tackled them from a slightly different angle; she found new strategies for dealing with them and she was proud of the fact. She exercised what freedom she had in each restricted situation. Once repetition is accepted, a small do-able change can take the place of something that is a large-scale, impossible endeavor.

And yet the Sisyphus problem still reappeared, this time from another quarter. Whereas her labor of Sisyphus at first entailed overcoming external aspects of life, in conquering the paradox of having to begin all over again and never really coming to an end, this woman then speaks of "inner problems," of struggles within herself that always made life difficult and which still exert the same kind of sway. Putting up with her own peculiarities and being able to tolerate herself—being able to bear her own difficult sides—this is what is meant here by the term "a labor of Sisyphus."

The seventy-three-year-old teacher alludes to something similar when he says that these days he sees the Sisyphus theme in terms of its connection with death. To a certain extent, he identifies with Sisyphus who had to roll the stone his whole life long: tackling tasks he was given, taking on the travails of life, not running away. Yet now he questions whether or not he has done the right thing. What does he mean when he says that he "shouldered the stone"? At the time, he thought he was doing his duty and today he feels that there are times when one could just as well leave the stone lying where it is. If one takes the more radical view, then the stone could be seen not only as a symbol of duty, but also as a symbol of all the difficulties of individual existence. This would mean that giving up the stone implies giving up one's own life, capitulating. This was not something that he had considered.

This is clear from the fact that he liked to think back on his job. It was a job which called for lots of repetition, a job which demanded a great deal of flexibility in the repetition. It was a job that called not so much for the repetition of subject matter, but rather for a love of teaching, the desire never to slack off but to always want to show new students interesting things, even if this meant repetition for the teacher. The drive for repetition demands creativity within the repetition. Repetition is just one structural element of existence, one that recognizes death. But what comes to light by virtue of repetition is the important thing. For the teacher, things only seemed like a labor of Sisyphus when he was discouraged or when he wanted too much.

This makes it clear that a labor of Sisyphus is not just pointless. Quite to the contrary: work can become a labor of Sisyphus at times when it seems particularly difficult, whether because our expectations are too high or—as is perhaps here the case—because we place inordinate demands on ourselves. We expect, for example, to work inspired by an uninterrupted love of teaching and to be perpetually inspired even within a continual cycle of repetition. Besides, Sisyphus didn't once push the stone down the hill; he just let it roll! In the case of the teacher, however, one gets the impression that he was thoroughly resigned to pushing the stone. In hindsight, he should have simply given himself greater freedom.

These impressions, drawn from people of all different ages, have given us some perspectives on the various experiences associated with the myth. The myth seems to have a lot to do with overcoming everyday reality. However, this burden can also be seen in our relationships. It is the burden of behavior that never changes, the burden that we mutually bear as a result of living with one another. Finally, the burden can be seen as part of having to put up with our own difficult sides. All these impressions make it clear that life includes the structural element of repetition. Lacking trust, we pose questions about the principle of repetition: we ask whether or not it is necessary or whether it arises out of our fear of change. This repetition has a lot to do with simple everyday life, with the awareness that we do not have to scale the highest peaks all the time; "peak experiences" are not always our preserve. Of course the older we get the more often we repeat things. It is after all a product of time. It would seem that people in mid-life have a considerably harder time with this than do older people. For forty-somethings the first awareness of aging is painful because so much is repeated and it is in this very repetition that we so often must start all over again. Also associated with the Sisyphean is always the question of the meaningfulness of what we do.

Certain tasks seems Sisyphean whenever we want too much, when we are too bound to the absolute and are unable to accept the finality of our own existence. It is in the dynamic of thwarted great expectations that we experience the sufferings of Sisyphus.

Reflections on the Mythical Image

Yes, I also got a glimpse of Sisyphus,
who slaved away in suffering;
he pushed a huge block
with both hands.
In truth, he pushed it up to the top
and leaned against it,
using his feet and hands; yet it was so far up
that the height
finally got the better of him and the load pushed
him backwards.
Then the shameless stone rolled back down again.
But again he started to slave away and pushed
so that his body was dripping with sweat
and around his head there was a cloud of dust.[2]

One can well imagine the scene. For me what predominates is the impression of "stoniness." The impression of great human effort and will exerted upon the stone is what sticks in my mind. The effort, the need to let go, and the determination with which Sisyphus keeps applying himself to the stone are essential to this text by Homer.

Using both hands and feet to push the stone, Sisyphus toils, his body dripping with sweat, his head enveloped by a cloud of dust.

It is an image of the most intense concentration and the greatest presence—which is probably why Sisyphus cannot pay attention to anything other than this stone and the effort involved in moving it. In this situation Sisyphus must focus on himself very intensely, just as we focus on ourselves when we completely concentrate on a task and are at one with it. We feel powerful and totally centered because we are not looking at ourselves. This is the kind of moment in which we can grow out of ourselves. It is a feeling of being at one with oneself and for oneself—an experience of being oneself in the moment of self-forgetting.

Sisyphus has no spectators: this part of the myth is not concerned with people admiring him; it isn't a narcissistic demonstration of power, in the sense of, "Hey, take a look at this . . ." It is a battle that he must overcome all by himself. Just before he reaches his goal, however, the extreme weight of the stone pushes him backwards and all the hope contained in this concentrated effort is thwarted. Right before the finish line, just when it is most trying and where it happens most often, he fails. Does Sisyphus think of his goal too soon, as we so often do, thus letting our concentration falter?

Perhaps it isn't really about getting the stone to the finish line. Perhaps it is his goal to concentrate as fully as possible and to see how far he can push the stone. Perhaps it has more to do with the process, in all its intensity, and less to do with attaining a goal?

We know that the stone will never reach the goal—at least in the myth. In reflecting upon this we are confronted with our own fears that ultimately our endeavors will fail, that everything might simply be in vain: meaningless, absurd, for nought. This is what compels us to seek a meaning in this apparently meaningless myth.

It is curious that there is no mention of Sisyphus having any reaction to the stone's rolling back down the hill again. The stone is deemed shameless and impudent. And at something of a loss, we ask why the stone should be ashamed—for its extreme heaviness perhaps? Yet from Sisyphus we hear nothing.

But what is contained in that moment when the stone rolls down into the fields? I imagine that Sisyphus leaps aside, breathing heavily, stands still, exhales, and then strides down into the valley after the stone.

Hurried? Reflective? Unburdened? Does he perhaps even notice his surroundings? Is his step like that of someone in touch with the stone and the rock, perhaps in tune with the landscape? About all this Homer says nothing. The phase of unburdening is unimportant. What is important is the phase of pressing forward, the phase in which Sisyphus shoulders the load over and over again. However, when we interpret the myth, then we are also at liberty to examine things differently than those who transcribed the myth.

Homer speaks of a rock that Sisyphus has to push up what is in all likelihood a mountain, since there is reference made to a summit. This rock is depicted on classical vases as being round, as a ball, and sometimes as a stone block—all of which are simply various different interpretations of the myth. In comparison with the human being, Sisyphus, these blocks or stones are always depicted as disproportionately large, and it is a wonder that any human being could even move such an object.

Stones as we find them in nature are just there; if they have to be moved, then they have to be moved by external means. Since a stone's hardness, solidity, angularity, and weight are all factors that work against us, it is often really difficult to get a

stone in motion, let alone rolling. But over and over again Sisyphus is able not only to move the stone, but also to roll it. Only
the goal prescribed by the myth—getting the stone to the summit—eludes him. But this, too, is a perspective that calls for
another interpretation. Such interpretations obtrude because
we see only the senselessness of always having to start from the
beginning. Yet it is just the torturousness of this situation that
frees us to experience the dimensions of the myth that are not
immediately addressed. Nevertheless, the myth is primarily concerned with failure, and Sisyphus does not, may not, cannot
give up. He tries over and over again from the beginning and
always reapplies himself to the task. Is he stubborn, compulsive,
or hopeful? Is he imbued with faith in himself, or is he simply
filled with stubbornness? Is he a symbol of the obstinacy that
causes us to want to achieve seemingly hopeless things? Or is he
also a symbol of the fact that our intentions and desires are
never proportionate to our power, despite all tenacity? Is Sisyphus a model of human excess, a model of a person who knows
no moderation, who is also impudent?

Johann Wolfgang von Goethe speaks to a similar issue in a
passage in his *Maxims and Reflections*:

> The most wonderful lunacy is that which relates to our-
> selves and to our own power, the fact that we dedicate our-
> selves to an undertaking, an honorable task that we are
> not up to, and that we strive towards a goal that we can
> never attain. The Tantalus–Sisyphus torture is what we
> experience as a result, and all the more bitterly the more
> honestly we try. And in fact just when we see ourselves
> eternally distanced from the thing that we are seeking, is
> very often the moment when we have already found
> something else worthwhile along the way, something fit-
> ting, something that we are actually born to enjoy.[3]

Clearly for Goethe it is the lack of moderation and the fact that
we overestimate ourselves that cause our Tantalus–Sisyphus

sufferings. It is interesting that he brings the Greek mythological figures of Tantalus and Sisyphus together here. Tantalus, Sisyphus and Prometheus are the famous penitents of the Underworld. Tantalus tests the omniscience of the gods by presenting them with his son as a meal. As a punishment he must suffer eternal hunger and thirst in the underworld. Though there is a tree laden with fruit just above him, it moves out of reach each time he reaches toward the branches. Beneath him is a lake which also moves away whenever he tries to scoop water from it. Tantalus must suffer eternal hunger and thirst, just as Sisyphus must struggle with his stone for all eternity. Tantalus, Sisyphus, and Prometheus all measured themselves against the gods, tried to prove themselves superior—and for this they were punished.

Perhaps the myth of Sisyphus also symbolizes the fact that despite all striving, as human beings we can never really complete something. Tasks can never be concluded, because life must keep going as long as we are alive.

If the myth tells us that no matter how much we struggle, ultimately we won't get anywhere, then we might ask why Sisyphus doesn't simply give up. The myth tells us that it is his punishment that he cannot give up.

The First Example: The Test That Has To Be Taken Over and Over Again

A man who is not a kid anymore really wants to take a test in a subject area in which he is not particularly talented. He complains and tortures himself, sometimes getting sick before the start of the test; he's already flunked twice, and he can only try one more time. He is asking too much of himself, but he doesn't want to admit this, cannot admit this. Like Sisyphus, he starts over and over again from the beginning with an incredible tenacity.

From an external point of view, he seems completely fixated on the idea of passing this exam. Nothing else interests him, not even the subject matter. All he is concerned with is the idea of passing the exam. He comes across as stubborn and extremely compulsive. When he fails he chides all the people who let him fail, denouncing them for their stupidity. Two days later, he pulls out his notes again. He wants to show everyone he can do it, that he has been treated unfairly. He doesn't want to give up; he probably cannot give up without forfeiting his own self-image and plunging into a deep crisis over his own self-worth.

The Second Example: The Picture That Must Be Painted Over and Over Again

A painter wants to paint a picture that she sees in her mind's eye, a picture that is very important to her. She paints the picture. To the observer, the picture is very evocative, yet to her it doesn't correspond to the image she has in mind. She paints another, and then another, and another. From an external point of view, her efforts seem compulsive. She is obsessed with the idea of representing her inner image in all its radiance as a physical entity. She suffers so from the fact that she is unable to do so that she becomes physically ill—and she paints on. She suffers from the fact that she is not free to do anything else—and hopes to find the right moment. Here we have something that resembles a creative obsession. The woman has enough energy to start over and over again, to stick with the same topic simply because she hopes that she will be successful, yet also because she suffers this incredible pressure from her psyche to paint this and no other picture. She is totally gripped by

the idea, just like the student who is gripped by the idea of passing the exam.

And yet there is a distinction to be made here. Even though
in this instance I characterized the student's perseverance as
stubbornness, I would never characterize the painter's perseverance as stubbornness, because in her case there always exists the
abiding hope that something will change. This is not the case
with the student. He covers a lot of ground in the attempts he
makes, does in fact do a lot of work, but it is a torture to him,
and he is not really enriched by what he learns. For the painter
on the other hand, though none of the paintings may be the
ultimate expression of what she wants to say, each picture
expresses something and she learns something from each picture. She states this when she says, "I'm making great progress in
the way I express myself. Each picture also teaches me something. I'm just not successful in painting *the* picture."

Does Sisyphus represent someone who neither can nor
wishes to let go once he has made up his mind to do something;
someone who despite hard work comes across as stubborn,
someone for whom the process means nothing and the goal
everything? Someone who for this very reason is unable to
attain the goal, someone whom we scrutinize and judge, and
whose hopes we put down? Or does Sisyphus instead represent
someone who is seized by an idea, someone who wants to
express this idea, someone who consistently and with incredible
persistence sticks to the job, someone who has both the process
and the goal in sight—and from an external point of view,
someone to whom we ascribe the phrase "legitimate hope"?

The difference would seem to be small, and yet it is enor-
mously large. In the case of the student, the stone that he has
taken on really is too large. In the case of the painter, the stone
may also be too large, but she grows with her stone, and with this

her art grows, too, as she over and over again makes renewed attempts. And even if it seems as though she might be doing the same thing repeatedly, there is in fact something that is always different. We can articulate this with a mythological image: both the stone and the journey that she undertakes with the stone—rolling the stone up the hill—symbolize change. This change may be imperceptible from one attempt to the next, but it is thoroughly evident if one looks at the attempts as a whole.

And if we choose to look at Sisyphus's stone as a real stone, then of course we can see that it, too, will be altered over time. It will be worn down by friction, and thanks to its altered shape and momentum, it will roll by different routes down the hill.

Both of the people in the examples I have given are similar insofar as they both are unable to free themselves from their stones; they have to keep on pushing them. At the moment this is using up all their energy and they are not at liberty to distance themselves. However, at the same time both of them experience their predicaments not as senseless, but rather as very meaningful.

Still, from an external point of view, it would seem as though one of the undertakings is senseless, stubborn, and thus ought to be abandoned, while the other is meaningful. This judgment is closely associated with whether or not we are able to see hope or hopelessness in a given situation. Linked to this is also the question of whether the effort incorporates the experiences that are gleaned along the way, or alternatively, whether it is just the goal that is important—whether there is a certain hope that things might change.

Hope and Hopelessness;

Or, Expectation and Disappointment

People have always reflected on hope and hopelessness when it comes to this part of the Sisyphus myth, Albert Camus did so, for example, in his book, *The Myth of Sisyphus. An Exploration of the Absurd.* For him, Sisyphus is a tragic and absurd hero. He knows the punishment of the gods and the rolling of the stone, and he knows that he won't have any success. He does not hope for mercy, does not believe in the gods; he is hopeless—without either hope or illusion—and nonetheless he rolls the stone. However, in so doing, he takes his fate into his own hands and ultimately refuses to be defeated by the gods. Being without hope or illusions also means being without a future. Sisyphus lives totally in the here and now—without asking for reward, with the "clandestine joy" that his fate belongs to him: "His stone is his own affair."[4]

Let's follow Camus's line of reasoning for a moment. Hidden behind all this exertion there is no meaning that would provide some reward, no better future to be gained through hard work. That would be just an illusion. But although it may be an illusion,

Sisyphus does not flee. Camus's book for the most part deals with the question of whether or not one should commit suicide in the face of the absurd. Fleeing would be tantamount to committing suicide. Sisyphus does not flee: he shoulders the stone.

And therein lies his dignity. He does not give up, doesn't flee, but stays responsible for his task. No god makes him responsible for it, but he himself, and he takes responsibility primarily for the part of the task over which he does have some control. This is one of the central tenets of French existentialism, and something that is already preempted in the epigraph with which Camus prefaces his book:

> Dear soul, do not strive
> for eternal life
> instead exhaust all possibilities.
> —Pindar, *Third Pythic Ode*

This attitude stands in opposition to the attitude that promotes flight, a flight into illusion, into death. Naturally human beings are predisposed to fleeing, and there are a concomitant number of myths and fairy stories in which gods and goddesses, heroes and heroines are in flight. The Sisyphus myth is not, however, a myth about someone fleeing. It is a myth about someone who holds his ground, who gives his all.

However, by virtue of the fact that the universe doesn't recognize any master, Camus further argues that Sisyphus accepts the punishment, doesn't grovel for mercy and doesn't run away, and that this universe is "neither barren nor worthless,"[5] (an odd argument if we consider that Sisyphus is, of course, still being punished by the gods, the very gods that Camus has dispensed with): "Every grain of this stone, every fragment of this mountain alone means an entire world to him. The struggle against the summit may well be fulfilling. We have to imagine Sisyphus as a happy person."[6]

Camus's point about the myth opens up a fascinating view of Sisyphus as the model of a person who, even though his situation was intended as a punishment, fulfills the obligation that has been prescribed, yet does so without hope of success or change. As such, Sisyphus would be a symbol for all those people who cannot foresee any change, and simply do whatever is at hand, yet still remain resolute in the hope that at some point fate will improve their lot. Are we surprised by such heroism? Do we even admire it? Upon closer examination, such heroism proves problematic.

According to Camus, it is not just his devotion to the seemingly hopeless task at hand that motivates Sisyphus, but rather the chance to displace the gods. In comparing himself to them, he proves that he is stronger. Examined from the point of view of depth psychology, we have before us someone who accomplishes a task by mustering up all of his ego power and giving it everything he has. On the other hand, such a person can never be weak, can never entertain any other thoughts or enjoy anything other than the struggle. This is a person who overexerts completely in order to show that he or she can do things alone, can do whatever he or she decides, and for whom unconscious tendencies never thwart conscious intentions. It is someone who always has everything under control—and yet who fails over and over again.

If we regard Sisyphus as a prototype for humanity, as he is viewed by French existentialism (at O. F. Bollnow's instigation[7]), then this mythical image quite clearly reveals the strengths and weaknesses of existentialism. The strength comprises the ability to stick to something, not to give up, and not to let either a god or anyone else be the master of one's fate. Responsibility for oneself, without reference to any kind of success is clearly a priority. Whatever fate may dole out, human beings still have the option of changing things. People should do whatever seems possible—a statement that is fundamental for psychotherapists who frequently find themselves dealing with clients who, in learning to understand that their current behavior has something to do with childhood experiences, continually try to make their fathers or mothers or fate itself "responsible" for their present difficulties—and, in so doing, push the principle of self-responsibility into the background. When this is the case, the idea behind French existentialism can function as a corrective: we must do whatever lies in our power in order to change our lives.

The weakness of French existentialism is revealed by that which is absent from the myth: The myth of Sisyphus is a thoroughly unerotic myth, lacking the whole dimension of love and interpersonal relationships. Missing too, is the capacity to be able to let go, of surrendering and trusting in something other than one's own power and one's own will. What is left out is the whole realm of the metaphysical and of hope. It is not by chance that at roughly the same time that Camus published his Sisyphus book, Gabriel Marcel[8] brought out his *Philosophy of Hope*. As opposed to Camus's exclusive emphasis on the here and now and the capacity of the human spirit, Marcel stresses trust, hope, and the mystery of love. As such, hope becomes the antithesis of arrogance and obstinacy. Camus and Marcel demonstrate two different aspects of humanity. Each position can be central in a given life situation, but it seems to me that both positions together—the very tension between them—constitute the essence of what it means to be human.

If, in his interpretation of the Sisyphus myth, Camus were to refer only to the fact that human beings are ultimately damned to an absurd fate by the gods—that they take on this fate, work at it, and thereby defy the gods (although to me this

would seem inordinately difficult without any hope of amelioration)—basically there would be little to object to in this. There
are phases in the lives of all of us during which we must function
in this mode, phases in which it is just this kind of attitude that
gives us the strength to live with our fate. Pitting ourselves
against our fate might also provide us with the first opportunity
to experience our own strength.

But when Camus adds that we should also conceive of Sisyphus as a happy person, I wonder why he bothers to introduce
this category. Were he to say that he views Sisyphus as one who
lives with the greatest intensity (*vivre le plus*), who really dares
to live, I would happily go along with his argument. But happy?
Wouldn't "worthy" be the more appropriate expression? By this
I don't mean to mount either a defense or a critique of existentialism as represented by Camus—for that I am concentrating
on far too narrow a text—but rather to find out whether Sisyphus is or was a happy person. Above all I am concerned with
questions of hope and hopelessness.

This seems to me to be an absolutely central issue, just as I
consider hope and hopelessness to be emotions central to
human life. Naturally hope always opens up the prospect of the
future, of change, and concomitantly also of creative change.
Hope lends us wings, comforts us, yet sometimes it leads us to
accept things too easily and prevents us from doing what is really possible. Perhaps we just hope that things will be different
and don't actually change what needs to be changed. From time
to time this brings discredit to hope.

However, hope is not about timidly waiting for a "perhaps,"
nor is it the building of castles in the air. Ultimately, hope is the
trust that something in life will carry us forward, that life in its
entirety and individual intentions can somehow be reconciled.
In hope there lies a kind of security. Hope also transcends the

here and now, transcends one's conscious will. Normally, hope gives us the strength to take something on, all the while trusting that something will change or at the very least that perservering has some purpose.

And Sisyphus is supposed to have accomplished this tremendous feat of strength, despite all of his failures, without any feeling of hope? If we consider Camus's argument more closely, it transpires that he doesn't actually wind up with no sense of hope. To be sure, Sisyphus knows that he will never reach the end—and since he is in the Underworld the repetition really is to be considered "eternal"—he has in other words no illusions. Yet he draws his "happiness" from the fact that he triumphs in his struggle with the summit. In so doing, it is the task he is engaged in and the experience of his own strength in a process that has no meaning which become fundamental. Nor does Camus's Sisyphus appear to be hopeless: he places hope in his own strength.

Ultimately we will never know whether Sisyphus was a person with or without hope. Today the myth has to be enriched with our own existential reflections. Nonetheless, I think that Sisyphus could not simply have been a person who bore this eternal repetition without hope . That seems to me to be an idea that demands too much of human beings.

I could imagine that Sisyphus does indeed acknowledge that the gods have told him that he will never reach the goal, yet that he still secretly hopes that he will reach it after all. He is challenged, summoned by this pronouncement, just as we are sometimes prompted to do something out of sheer perversity when we meet with a downright rejection of our capabilities. It is the manifestation of heroic hope in the face of contradiction. As we all know, stubbornness is a very important human strength. Quite frequently we make progress out of sheer obstinacy, in response to an unflattering statement that someone has made about us. By being obstinant we often discover all of the possibilities that are available to us, and finally we stick up for ourselves. Sisyphus is a stubborn hero. Viewed in this light, Sisyphus's struggle is a conflict with fate, with the gods, but also a conflict that is much more open than the one postulated by Camus: Sisyphus does not despise the gods, he just measures himself against them.

His perserverence and dignity are demonstrated by the fact that he has to continually reconcile himself to being thwarted.

Thus the point is not that mankind lives on in the face of hopelessness, accepts absolute finiteness, achieves as much as possible in life, and ultimately scorns death. The point is rather that mankind hopes, strives, and suffers repeated disappointment, and yet in spite of these disappointing setbacks does not flee, but keeps on trying, and thereby also steals a piece of life from death.

In other words, in being disappointed, we have to leave behind the preconceptions that we had: we expected something that has not come to pass. We didn't hope for something, we expected it. Expectation is much narrower than hope, much more fixated on a specific occurrence. If the expected does not come about, then we lose our equilibrium. The feeling that accompanies this loss is what we call disappointment. The sense of disappointment is often what makes us aware of what we have actually been expecting all along, and that this expectation has not been fulfilled, and perhaps cannot be fulfilled. Then the important question arises as to how we are supposed to deal with the feelings of disappointment.

Sisyphus is the model of a person who in spite of his disappointment continues to make an effort, who shoulders the stone again, who wants to wipe out the sense of loss and reapply himself to the task. Someone else in the same situation as Sisyphus

might stay at the top of the mountain and complain, even if she
had already been told beforehand that she would be disappointed. It would be difficult for someone like this to start over again:
she would be afraid of being disappointed yet again. Sisyphus on
the other hand, is able to defiantly process the disappointment
and the associated insult. He doesn't let the feeling of disappointment hinder him in his desire to conquer life; as such he
wrests a bit of life from death. But Sisyphus is not just a hero
who is difficult to offend, he is also a very powerful hero, a hero
with lots of energy.

The myth does not address the issue of his disappointment.
We hear nothing about the way he makes his way down the hill
to the fields—which might give us some indication of how he
experiences and processes his feelings of disappointment. The
myth says only that he begins anew. To the extent that we want
to identify with him, he also gives us courage to make a new
start at things, even in those instances when it is the self-same
burden that must be born.

If we look at this myth not from the point of view of hope
and hopelessness, but rather from the aspect of expectation and
the associated disappointment, then the heroic act of Sisyphus
is not diminished, and he can no longer be viewed as an absurd
hero. Living life means taking the plunge over and over again,
even though one knows that ultimately disappointment is
always a possibility. It means accepting and seeing things in a
broader context, that one has to continually let go of expectations and preconceptions, yet at the same time, not give up. Of
course, we all know just how much energy this takes, and also
how much courage.

Repeated Disappointments and New Hope

What comes to mind in this context are relationships. This
is one area where we have many expectations, and where many

of these expectations are also disappointed. If we don't want to keep getting disappointed and getting stuck in the role of victim, but would rather learn how to enter into new relationships—albeit with the certainty that some disappointments will result, perhaps even the same ones—then we must constructively realize Sisyphus.

An especially powerful illustration of this point appears in Ingeborg Bachmann's story, "Undine Goes." Undine settles her score with men. In so doing, it transpires that for her all men have the same name, have the same desires, that with each successive man everything always starts over from the beginning:

> You people! You monsters!
> You monsters with the name Hans! With the name I can never forget.
> Whenever I came through the clearing and the branches parted, when the birch branches flicked the water off my arms, the leaves lapped the drops from my hair, I came across someone who was called Hans.
> Yes, this fact I have learned, that someone has to be called Hans, that you are all so named, one and alike, and yet are only one person. Always only one it is, who bears this name, whom I cannot forget, even when I forget you all, totally forget how I loved you. And when your kisses and your sperm have long since been rinsed off and washed away by the many great waters—rain, river, sea— the name still remains. It continues to grow under water because I cannot stop calling it, Hans, Hans. . . .[9]
> To be no where, to stay no where. To dive, to rest, to move without the slightest exertion—and one day to remember, to re-emerge, to come through a clearing, see him and say, "Hans." To begin with the beginning.
> "Hello."
> "Hello."
> "How far is it to you?"
> "It is far, far."
> "And it is far to me."
> To keep on repeating a mistake, to make a mistake that distinguishes one.[10]

In relationships one keeps on making the same mistake, a mistake "that distinguishes one." This wonderful expression refers to the fact that these mistakes mark us, and yet also distinguish us; it is in other words, our characteristics that give us a very particular meaning.

And obviously Undine laspses into making the mistake that distinguishes her. Having settled her score with the monsters, she says:

> But I can't go on like this. So let me say something good to you again, so that things won't be so divided. So that nothing will be divided.[11]

Here too the problematic nature of this behavior becomes apparent. Situations can arise in which a person lapses directly into the compulsion to repeat, spends an enormous amount of energy trying to reach the same point over and over again, perhaps being unable to stop rolling the very same stone, with the same amount of force and using exactly the same strategies.

An Example:
Foolish Expectations

A man married a seriously depressed woman. He made it his life's work to alleviate her depression. At the same time he was able to delegate his own depressive tendencies to her and also to fight them in her. He spoiled her, did everything for her, humored her, inspired her. Sometimes he felt really bad because his own needs were not being taken into consideration. And time and time again his wife told him that she simply could not go on. Each time he was very disappointed, but he did not let on and instead came up with new ideas, tortured himself even more, thought that he had to succeed. But of course he simply could not succeed. Living with him like this, his wife was unable to put herself to the test; she was unable to get any stronger or to put herself into the position of being able to roll her own stone.

I have included this example here because I want to show that Sisyphus's behavior really is not something that can be appropriately implemented all the time. It has to be implemented in the right time and place. Having the courage to start again, which also means having the courage to accept loss, can at the same time simply be a compulsion to repeat things, a blind desire to get one's own way. It can be an expression of the fact that one is unable to give up, that one does not want to give up.

The Stone as Symbol

The stone has symbolic value not only as something that offers resistance, as some opposition. It is not just representative of a burden, or of absence. The solidity and near immutability of the stone make it a symbol of steadiness and permanence as well—and reliability, to which the whole constellation of "resistance" belongs. Only something that offers resistance is so firm that we can depend on it if we must.

This myth then is part of the construct associated with steadiness, immutability, and reliability.

Because of their indestructability, steadiness, and reliability, stones are also regarded as symbols of the divine and of concentrated divine power. Particularly meteorites, stones that "fall from the sky" and come from the cosmos, have always been seen as an expression of the proximity of the heavens to the earth, and thus have been associated with fertility. Incidentally, in Greek antiquity long before the gods were represented in human form, an unhewn stone was the symbol of Hermes or Apollo.[12]

Initially, it would seem as though our myth only deals with the resistant, obstructionary, burdensome qualities of the stone, those which demand enormous effort from anyone who wants to confront the obstacle. Nevertheless, I think it is important that we don't lose sight of the wider symbolism, which views the stone as representative of the divine. As such, there shouldn't be just the implicaton of burden and effort. The effort should also have some meaning. It should embody aspects of the divine, as should each and every undertaking in life.

Were this Hermes rather than Sisyphus, then the symbol would certainly point to creativity and transformation, for Hermes is the god who protects gates and doors, wanderers and border-crossers, but also who shows the way to the Underworld. He is endowed with a capacity for invention and trickery. In other words, he is also a god who is responsible for transition, metamorphosis, and transformation. At first glance, a god who is responsible for change would seem to be the direct antithesis of Sisyphus. We will return to Hermes shortly.

Were the symbolic reference to Apollo, on the other hand, there would be several possibilities for interpretation. Apollo has often changed his meaning. Originally also a gate-keeper, he increasingly became a god of salvation and atonement. Later his son Asklepios took over the function of healing. Nonetheless Apollo is still closely associated with healing is his capacity for wisdom; he addresses human beings through his oracle. Since the sixth century before Christ, Apollo has also been honored as Helios, the sun, who is not only the god of light but also one who maintains order. He is a god of correct proportions.[13]

The themes of salvation and atonement might also be ones which Sisyphus is burdened with symbolically. Associated with this are the Apollonian analogies of wisdom, correct proportions, and the eternally rising sun.

The myth of Sisyphus did not appear in early antiquity. The expanded interpretation which I have included here is thus only admissable if one accepts that in certain circumstances earlier forms of expression are appropriated by later myths. What I am mainly concerned with here is pointing out that a human being doesn't just bear a burden, but rather that this burden must also be seen as a kind of task. In Greek times this was associated with the burden of a god—a struggle that could ultimately help someone attain something of the divine.

What remains, in spite of this expanded interpretation, is that in the eyes of his chroniclers at least, Sisyphus did not meet with success. He tried and tried—without end and without liberation. As such, his "success" lies in perpetual effort and only in this.

However, now the matter doesn't seem so meaningless anymore. Sisyphus does what is humanly possible to accomplish the life-task that has been accorded him. More than this he cannot do. He cannot complete the task in the truest sense of the word. All he can do is stick at it. However, now it is a different kind of sticking-power. Now it is associated with hope, the hope for meaning. He doesn't simply bear a burden, but has a task that brings him into conjunction with the divine. Yet the meaning in this interpretation lies not in the fact that the task will be completed, but rather in the distance that is covered with this "stone," with the experiences that one has along the way. In Sisyphus's case, this is the experience of strength and of power.

It is possible to interpret the story by viewing the stone as a burden or simply someone's lot in life, but there are other ways of looking at it too. Here the interpretation prompts the following questions: Do we want to view the rock, the pushing of the stone as an all-too-human situation? Do we want to understand the stone simply as an immobile burden, one that merely encumbers, provides trouble, and senselessly demands all of our strength? Or do we want to find life-tasks embodied in the stones that we bear—even though they are sometimes unpleasant?

Don't we perhaps want to find the hidden meaning? Perhaps even to sometimes invent one?

These two possibilities for interpretation are linked: lurking in the greatest problems that we face is also our greatest potential for development. Our problems constantly place demands on us and in so doing, they force us to grow.

Now it occurs to me that we have to take into consideration one aspect that is always touched upon in our dealings with the myth: a task doesn't so much depend on reaching a goal as it does on being involved in a journey, though obviously a path leads toward a goal. It is not attaining the goal that is important, but rather the fact that we apply ourselves to the journey and that have the courage to start anew each time.

The Preconditions
for the Punishment

The First Part of the Myth of Sisyphus

Having dealt at such length with Sisyphus's punishment, since the punishment is so much more germane than the little-known background story, the question arises as to why Sisyphus was actually punished in the first place. This background story will shed light on some of the interpretative themes that we have dealt with thus far.

W. H. Roscher has pointed out that in translation Sisyphus simply means "the cunning one." According to *The Iliad* (6: 152), Sisyphus was numbered as one of the most cunning, wily people who lived in Corinth in one corner of Argos.

All the things that he is supposed to have done, according to legend, seem rather confusing. I include here the full entry from *The Dictionary of Myth and Figures of Antiquity*:

Sisyphus, son of Aeolus and Enarete. He founded the city of Corinth, which he originally called Ephyra. His cunning and skill were legendary. For this reason he is sometimes associated with the master thief Autolykos (irrespective of myth chronology). Later historians maintain that Autolykos stole his herd, and that later Sisyphus won them back. Before they were stolen, Sisyphus had scratched grooves into their hooves and was thus able to disprove Autolykos's protestations to the contrary. He then took revenge on the thief by seducing his daughter Antikleia—thus the occasional rumor that Sisyphus and not her husband Laërtes was the father of Odysseus, whom she later bore.

When Sisyphus founded Ephyra, he created the Isthmis Games there in honor of Melikertes, whose body he found and buried there. He also fortified the adjacent heights of the Acrocorinth, making a citadel and watch tower. One day he happened to see Zeus abducting the water nymph Aigina, the daughter of the river god Asopos and Metope; Zeus carried her to the island Oinone, where he raped her. Asopos took pursuit and asked Sisyphus for help. Sisyphus promised to tell him what he knew if Asopos would give him a fresh-water spring on the Acrocorinth. This Asopos immediately provided (the Pirene spring). Zeus was furious about Sisyphus's disclosure and wanted to punish him. He sent Thanatos (death) to take him to the house of Hades. Sisyphus, the cunning, outwitted Thanatos in some way or other, tied him up, and threw him into a dungeon, after which the mortals no longer died. The gods, who were completely unsettled by this unnatural turn of events, sent Ares to free Thanatos, who then sought out Sisyphus for a second time. This time, Sisyphus had given his wife, Pleiade Merope, precise instructions: she let his body lie unburied and she did not bring the body any of the usual sacrifices. In this way, Sisyphus outwitted Hades: the god was so infuriated by Merope's negligence that he or his wife Persephone let Sisyphus go back into the upper world in order to punish Merope and to occasion the burial of the body. Having returned to Corinth, Sisyphus did nothing of the sort. Instead he rejoiced in life and grew very old, laughing all the while at the gods. One would assume that it was probably because of his godlessness and his betrayal of Zeus that after his death his shade was tormented in Tartaros: he had to continually roll a huge stone up a hill, and when he had almost gotten it to the top, it always rolled down again.

After a long reign, Sisyphus was buried on the Isthmus [the long neck of land of Corinth]. He left behind four sons: Glaukos (father of Bellerophon), Ornytion (father of Phokos 2), Thersandros and Almos.[14]

Sisyphus's many deeds cited here are listed in all of the pertinent lexicons, although some emphasize different things. Central to all of them however, is his capacity to outwit death.

Looking at all of his deeds, one might easily be convinced that Sisyphus must indeed have been an extraordinarily cunning, skillful, clever, and courageous man. He fought with the gods; they had to reckon with him. From this, one might infer that, given his punishment in the Underworld, the gods are in fact the stronger. But is it just a simple power struggle between a man and the gods? Or does it symbolize how man's struggle with the gods can enrich his life—but how he ultimately may be punished for this?

Or are the mythmakers perhaps trying to construe a punishment and a justification, fearing that human beings after Sisyphus might become too arrogant, might call the gods into question, and in so doing, make themselves into gods—something that does not correspond to human limitations?

This would explain the fact that Sisyphus's cunning and misdeeds are described in such detail. An example is clearly being made of him, and the theme of human moderation is being proposed as a lesson.

Sisyphus — the Sneak
and the Trickster

Sisyphus must be a master thief in order to successfully outwit Autolykos, the master thief himself, and win back his cattle. Autolykos, in turn, owes his knowledge to none other than Hermes, who had given him the gift of being able to make the dehorned cattle he stole look like horned cattle, and to make the white ones look like black ones, and vice versa.[15] Understanding Hermes thus helps explain part of the nature of Sisyphus. For this reason, we need to examine that god's own symbolic nature in detail.

To Hermes, piles of stone were sacred, as were tombs. The stone pillars, called *hermes,* that protected Greek houses were also regarded as his domain. Hermes was seen as a god who was continually on the move. As stated earlier in the discussion of Ali Baba, he was not only the god of travelers and wanderers, but also a divine messenger, linking earth and sky, and an envoy of the dead, linking the earth and the Underworld. Cunning is a significant aspect of his character. He, too, is described as a master thief, who when barely out of the womb had already stolen a herd of cattle from his brother Apollo. Lucky discoveries and the notion of "finders-keepers" are the preserve of Hermes. For this reason, he is also a god who makes lots of discoveries, and the god of those who make such discoveries. Naturally he is also responsible for discoveries at a spiritual level, for interpretation and explanation (hermeneutics). Aside from this, he is also supposed to have invented dice and the art of dice divination.[16] Because of all this, he is the patron saint of discoverers, intellectuals, orators, thieves, and business people. But he is also the god who sends people dreams and stimulates them to dream.

Hermes is one of the "divine children" of mythology. He expresses the recurring possibility of the new beginnings of all life, of an irrepressible life force. In addition, he harbors traces of a fertility god: his relationship to the stones in the fields may be an expression of a pre-Greek fertility cult. This would bring him into close connection with the Great Mother. He is at home in the real world, as well as in Heaven and in the Underworld. He is a god who creates the connections between things, who brings about transitions and thereby promises creative transformation. Because he is eternally roving, always in motion, he is and will stay a young god. He remains inexorably linked to the emotion of hope, with the certainty that everything will somehow find a solution. And since he is a god of the moment and of connections, the consequences of his deeds do not seem to trouble him.

As a master thief, he is able to show others how they too can become master thieves. In *Phaedrus*, Plato writes that every human being possesses a trait of a god and that by living in imitation of the god, so honors him.[17]

Therefore Sisyphus is without doubt someone who lives "under the sign" of Hermes, who leads a life that is clearly determined by the capabilities and peculiarities of this god. Naturally, this classical Greek way of thinking has long since been lost to us: Everyone has better or worse character traits, but when someone shows a clearly discernable predisposition for something, we are quick to define this as abnormal, if not downright sick. Perhaps we would be better able to deal with our own distinguishable peculiarities if we were able to see them as the workings of a god or as an expression of something that is absolutely necessary to human life.

Let us now take a closer look at the characteristics in Sisyphus that are determined by Hermes:

The Master Thief

We know the master thief from fairy stories. Clearly he is a figure who has long preoccupied us. In such fairy stories, he is invariably the wayward son who would rather play dumb tricks than do any work. He is chased away from home or goes off of his own accord. Many years later, he returns as an upstanding gentleman, who has made his fortune and now reveals his identity.

In one such folk tale, the master thief then goes to the local count, his godfather, and at the count's own bidding steals the count's best horse (by disguising himself as a woman and getting the servants drunk) and then the countess's bedsheet and wedding ring (by a complicated ruse involving a ladder, a corpse, and another disguise). The count then challenges the thief to lock the priest and the sexton of the neighboring congregation in the count's hen house without using any force. The master thief spends the whole day looking for crabs, then puts little burning lights between their pincers and sets them loose in the graveyard at night. Proclaiming that the end of the world is nigh—and that the proof is in the churchyard, he quickly tricks the priest and sexton into a large bag and delivers them to the henhouse The count finally bribes him to go to another land because he is too dangerous to keep around.[18]

This type of fairy story, with some small differences, is very widespread. If one can look at this fairy story without moralizing, then it becomes clear that the master thief is not primarily concerned with amassing wealth. He is more interested in having fun by outwitting others. And whoever is most cunning is the one who triumphs. These master thieves are extraordinarily inventive fairy-tale heroes. On the one hand, they have really creative ideas, and on the other, they are true masters of the art of cunning. They are able to project themselves into other people's minds and predict what they will do. It is all about competition, about a rivalry of creative impulses. That these master thieves also become rich in the process is just a lucky coincidence. Nevertheless, like Hermes, none of them have any place to call home. Over and over again, they have to move on, and in so doing, of course, learn a great deal.

Sisyphus proves not only that Autolykos, the master thief, is guilty of stealing, but that he himself is superior to the master thief: he leaves Autolykos squabbling with the witnesses and in the meantime seduces his daughter.[19] This seduction is alleged to have resulted in the birth of Odysseus, whose wanderings can now be understood as fated. Who ultimately was responsible for seducing whom in this case remains unclear.

Sisyphus would thus symbolize a person who has creative ideas but cheats other people. He would also be concerned with the quick creative act, one that brings about some change. He would be less concerned with the consequences. Certainly it would be easy to provoke him into using this cunning: Sisyphus cannot bear the fact that his herd has been stolen by Autolykos. Using all of the power at his disposal, he stands up for what belongs to him and he wins.

The Spring That Was Bargained For

Sisyphus sees Zeus abducting the daughter of the river god. Aesopos is searching for her, and Sisyphus is prepared to give him information in exchange for a spring on the hitherto waterless hill near Corinth, the Acrocorinth. He receives this spring, which is also associated with other origin stories. Here Sisyphus proves himself very adroit at bargaining: information in exchange for water. A spring on the waterless Acrocorinth must have had very great significance: water means life and fertility, not only for Sisyphus, but also for the whole city. He thus exploits the predicament of a god in order to gain something that would provide him and his countrymen with a better life. From a symbolic point of view, this act would also provide more liveliness. Sisyphus was simply at the right place at the right time; he was attentive.

If one examines this story at the symbolic level, then Sisyphus is prepared to betray the Olympian Zeus to the river god, the god of water, of eternal flow. In other words, he puts himself in his good graces. The river god's favor becomes manifest in the spring that flows from the earth. It represents the overflowing abundance of Mother Earth and is a symbol of fertility, of a lively feeling of abundance and riches. But in acquiring the spring, Sisyphus also gains Zeus as an enemy.

Sisyphus pays little heed to the displeasure of Zeus. As the highest god, Zeus is the lord of both gods and men; he demands obedience and crushes resistance. Sisyphus sets himself against Zeus. He does so not only by virtue of the fact that he does not concern himself with Zeus's demands, but also because he concerns himself with something that is useful and probably also thoroughly pleasurable to himself and the whole city he has founded. He is not interested in obedience, but in life. He does not want to be one of Zeus's attendants, but rather part of the retinue of a river god, who personifies eternal transformation, eternal flux: continual change.

If we were to view him as a model, Sisyphus would be attracted to eternal transformation, as he is so clearly represented in the image of flowing water. He is gripped by creative change. If Sisyphus is representative of the creative person, then expressed in this image he also symbolizes the fundamental conflict within every creative person. He cannot be creative and at the same time completely respect the old order, since everything creative also stands in opposition to the old order that it comes into conflict with it. No wonder then that Zeus feels challenged.

The draconian punishment shows how threatened Zeus feels by Sisyphus: he is supposed to die soon.

Death Outwitted

The motif of outwitting death is also one that we know well from fairy tales. In some variations Death is replaced by the Devil. By way of example, I would like to point out two types of fairy stories. One is represented by the French fairy tale "How Death Was Duped."

A saint gives a woman a free wish for her services. Her wish is that she might catch and punish everyone who climbs up her plum tree to get plums. The saint fulfills this strange wish. Ten years later, Death comes by her house and wants to take her with him. She says that she is prepared to go, but adds that before she goes she would like to be able to eat a couple of plums. Death climbs up the tree to fetch some plums for her. And the woman says, "I wish that Death can't get out of the tree without my permission."

Death flies into a passion, pleads, threatens, screams, but he can't get down again. And no one on earth can die. All of the infirm, injured, and sick suffer terribly because they are unable to die. People come from far and wide to ask the woman to let Death go. Finally she agrees on the condition that she must call Death three times before he comes to get her.[20]

This type of fairy story coincides well with the story of Sisyphus. Again it is a story in which cunning plays a great role, in which cunning and people's desires prevail over death, and transitoriness is overcome.

What is also clear from the example of this fairy story is what happens when Death is banished. Nothing can change, nothing can be brought to a conclusion, and this too brings suffering. Yet the secret pleasure probably consists in the knowledge that if one can't actually destroy Death, the indestructible destroyer,[21] then one can still banish him: an incredible triumph of human power over the law of life, over the gods. If the woman in the French fairy story disposes of Death thanks to a wish that she has been granted, and that she has also earned, then Sisyphus does something comparable with his cleverness and his physical strength. He puts Death out of commission; he does not accept the punishment that Zeus has intended for him. In so doing, he also annuls the principle of transitoriness, the other principle of the creative to which this inexorably belongs. Ares, the impetuous fighter among the gods, who is in the service of destructive change has to come to the aid of Death.

If we see Sisyphus as a model for human beings, then it is as a model of someone who is so convinced of his own strength, his intelligence, and his capacities for creativity, and who believes he is immortal. Death, change, having to let go, setbacks—none of these qualities exists for him. When the principle "Death" shows himself thus, Sisyphus ties him up and locks him away in a lumber room when he is threatened by him. However, in so doing, he makes himself into Zeus' equal, putting himself on the same footing as the gods, but he also nullifies the principle which enables the creative to exist. Ares, the god who embodies the principle of fighting and aggression, reverses the effects of this cunning move. The gods are superior to Sisyphus after all.

But this also means that death is efficacious after all, even for Sisyphus, if we conceive of death as a sign of impending old age, or if we see death as an aspect of things coming to an end— the other face of the creative. We shouldn't forget that Sisyphus followed the ever-youthful god Hermes, and he still follows him. He must thus fight against death, but he cannot completely deny the principle of destruction. And this is surely the reason he wants to outwit death a second time. This enables him to grow old.

Death Outwitted a Second Time

Here, too, Sisyphus demonstrates his capacity for far-sightedness. He knows what will happen and he can predict the reaction of the gods in the Underworld. He tells his wife not to bury the body and not to bring any sacrifices for the dead. This outrages the gods. By doing this, Sisyphus instructs his wife not to accept the gods of the Underworld and not to sacrifice anything to them. At Sisyphus's instigation, his wife neither recognizes nor accepts death, so the gods of the Underworld send Sisyphus back into the world in order to complain about her breaking the customs. Naturally he doesn't return to the Underworld after this mission but stays on the earth—and grows very old and laughs at the gods. Twice he has conquered death and proved himself sneakier than the gods. This derision of the gods stresses the fact that measuring oneself against the gods and proving oneself superior to them has a central function in this myth.

The cunning idea of refusing to make a sacrificial offering is, however, an idea he could only have implemented with the help of his wife. This is the only time that his wife is ever mentioned—otherwise she plays no role whatsoever in the myth. The "task" that Sisyphus takes on is to measure himself against the gods, particularly the god of death. Now Sisyphus can live in the world and grow old. He can laugh about the gods who are not prepared to do battle again. In and of itself it would be a simple feat to challenge Sisyphus again. Had the gods already lost their nerve? Or were they wise in trusting that for a mortal sooner or later the hour of death must toll?

We see something comparable to Sisyphus's cunning in the Icelandic fairy story, "Death and the Prince":

An unknown master promises to teach a king's son wisdom as no one else had been taught. The prince sits silently for three long years with a wise man in the forest and thus learns from a silent master. After three years have passed, the wise man reveals to him that he is Death and that depending on whether or not he sits by the bed of a sick person, the illness can be quick or slow, the sick person can recover or die. The master then gives him pointers about different remedies.

The prince becomes a famous doctor, then king, and when he is a hundred years old, one day he sees an old master sitting at his head, a sign that he is about to die. The king asks the master for a reprieve until he has said the Lord's Prayer. But he says only the first four verses and then explains that he will finish the prayer when he has finished living. Death has been outsmarted and has to leave him. After another hundred years the king grows tired of living, so he says the Lord's Prayer to the end and dies.[22]

Both types of fairy story that I have included here have something to do with outwitting Death and are linked by this common thread. The characters are concerned with proving themselves superior to death, which is nonetheless something that can only temporarily be achieved. Ultimately death is of course inexorable. But these are examples of postponing death until one is tired of life.

In the fairy tale "How Death Was Duped,"we have above all an example of how cunning can allow us to stave off death, and to ensure as much time—not to mention as much life intensity—as possible. This can be taken two ways: On the one hand, it implies our resolve in the face of unavoidable death: not to relinquish life too early, not to give up too soon, but rather to live life as fully as possible. We can see this death as dying, but also as the principle of transitoriness. Outwitting death can thus imply a refusal to surrender to such transitoriness, a refusal to give up too early, to stop rolling the stone too soon—if we are to put it in the language of the second part of the myth. But outwitting death can also mean then that we refuse life, with all its transitoriness and the associated necessity of having to let go and new beginnings. We refuse to accept the principle of repetition.

In the fairy story "Death and the Prince," as well as in the Grimm fairy story about Goodman Death,[23] it is a doctor who, having apprenticed himself to Death who was disguised as a mysterious wise man, is now dying but manages to outwit death. In other words, it is death itself that teaches us how to deal with it. The fairy story "Death and the Prince" also shows how every illness can also be regarded as existing in the presence of death, but a presence that need not lead to death. It seems to me that in this fairy story, Death demands of human beings that we defend ourselves against him. And Death even goes so far as to show us the means to do so.

However, in all such fairy tales Death also establishes clear limitations on the capacity of human beings to heal sickness. He expresses the notion of a kind of double standard with regard to life: on the one hand, there is an injunction to stay alive as long as possible; on the other, to accept that in certain circumstances there is no remedy we can take to stave off death. We simply have to let go. Naturally, in each case these doctors try and outsmart death. In the fairy tale about Goodman Death, the doctor quickly turns the patient's bed around, but in so doing, he himself dies. Even when these doctors become excessive in their use of the very skill that they have received from Goodman Death, and turn themselves into masters of life and death, ultimately it is still Death who establishes human moderation and rejects our claim to the absolute. Yet Death also seems to provoke cunning—he also accepts the fact that he may have been outwitted. It is in just this outwitting of Death that death is taken most seriously: it prompts us to make a great effort to keep life going. In the fairy story, however, Death can only be outwitted for a certain length of time, and this is also true for Sisyphus. Nonetheless, he can still live to a ripe old age. Then he too will die.

And Once Again
the Stone

The myth makes things quite explicit: because Sisyphus has outwitted death twice, his shade must roll the stone in the Underworld; he can never stop rolling the stone and yet it will always keep slipping away from him. This life-theme of having to stick to some task and yet always having to let go—and associated with it, the theme of eternal repetition—repeats itself here, renewing itself endlessly.

Sisyphus wanted to outwit death, to stop something from coming to an end, to prevent himself from having to let go. Now here in the shadow realm his suffering never comes to an end, and he cannot let go, cannot stop pushing the stone, and yet each time has to let go. His central life-theme is repeated in the world of the shades: the theme of not wanting to accept transience and yet of having to accept it. He still sets his will against having to give up, against this transience. Still he does not freely let go; he only lets go when the weight of the stone gets the better of him. He cannot let go and for this reason something is perpetually taken away from him. He keeps wanting to outwit death.

What in the world of the living still remained so playful and required little effort has now become the most terrible hardship.

Of course, Sisyphus reminds us of the situation in which many doctors find themselves. To a great extent, we delegate the responsibility of fighting death to doctors. It is not only the "last death" that they are supposed to prolong for as long as possible; whenever they can, they are also supposed to preserve eternal youth for us. They make every effort to fulfill these desires that we delegate to them, but in so doing, many doctors have to pay a price.

In comparing the fairy tales that I have chosen to illustrate the myth, what becomes clear is that ultimately we must choose when it makes sense to preserve this notion of "more life" and not let go, and when death must be accepted. We have to decide when it is time to consent to a loss and say goodbye. Sisyphus never agreed to this, and it is thus his punishment that now he can never give his consent. If we consider his life story, at least as much of it as we know, we have to conclude that we are dealing with someone who is concerned with winning, not losing, and who is so clever and cunning that he does not have to lose very often. Unlike Hermes, with whom he shares so many characteristics, Sisyphus lacks the quality of being an escort of the dead. He doesn't take any of the dead to the Underworld. He ties up Death and outwits him. An absolutely fearless fighter for more life, one who does not give up and is an incredibly determined hero, he is by the same token a prisoner of his resolve not to give up but always to fight against death.

The myth does not provide any answers: When does it makes sense to deny death? When should one be cunning and snatch life out of death's clutches, thereby making it precious? How long should we fight against transience and resignation? And, on the other hand, when should we just accept loss? The myth does not say, but it does provide an example, by illustrating in an analagous manner, what happens when we do not accept loss. Of course, we will not succeed in being as consistent as Sisyphus. But like Sisyphus, if we never consent to loss, then we will always be rolling a stone up the hill, and our stone will also get too heavy for us and roll down back into the valley, depriving us of all of our efforts.

An Example: The Refusal to Accept Loss

A forty-five-year-old man with lots of options open to him and blessed with the strength to pursue these things, complains that he feels overburdened. He says that he believes he is making every effort and yet achieving nothing that is really important to him. All he manages to achieve is routine work. He keeps working and everything gets to be too much for him, since actually he has the feeling that in spite of trying as hard as he can, somehow he's not doing it right. He thinks he should probably give up something, but doesn't want to. He's convinced that at some point all of his life options and capabilities will come together, and that this will then be the high point of his life.

This is a very prosaic example of how the myth of Sisyphus can be translated into our everyday lives. Like Sisyphus on his best days, this man probably has many life opportunities that he creates for himself. However, each opportunity that we follow up on is also going to have consequences. It is a point of departure for a chain of events that are mostly associated with work. There comes a day when the question of quitting arises, even though this is associated with loss. Quitting is however, exactly what this man doesn't want to deal with. After all, quitting means accepting that there are limitations to what we can do and recognizing that human life always verges on death. He is seized by the idea of attaining something really great in his life—of really and truly getting the stone to the top of the mountain. And because he cannot let anything go, the work load becomes increasingly heavy and he feels that he is getting further and further away from the "high point" for which he is striving. But like Sisyphus, he keeps pushing the stone, only with the more exhausted hope that by so doing he will have his peak moment, but more certain that he must sacrifice something to do so.

Another Example on the Same Subject

A forty-nine-year-old woman, just as highly talented, never has known quite what to do with her life. She is artistically talented in several different areas, yet she has a job that is not in the arts. She is unable to decide on one thing or the other: she lives for a few years making art, then returns to her old job, then turns back to art again. Relationships are indeed very important to her, but she doesn't want to settle down in a relationship.

She, too, now rolls a stone. She tortures herself about the meaning of life and then, just when she thinks that she has found some meaning, the stone escapes her again. This perpetual question about the meaning of life is consistent with her refusal to decide for—or against—things, and with her refusal to let many things die.

The student whom I mentioned earlier in this section cannot admit that he has failed in the subject area that he has chosen. So instead he has to burden himself with an ever-larger stone, one that he obviously can't push anymore.

This is what happens when we cannot accept that failure is a sign of our limitations, something that helps us to realistically estimate our capacities, to live a more moderate life, and to know our own measure. When we are not mindful of these things and are seized by the desire to make things better all the time, we overburden ourselves with our own demands and can even become paralyzed.

If we try to tease out the common thread in all of these examples, what emerges is that despite their differences and despite the fact that they experience their respective burdens differently, these people all suffer and do not find themselves in a position to change. So just as Sisyphus rolls his stone endlessly, they too roll their stones. They cannot escape their life situations and permit transformation. It may well be that they experience a fundamental crisis which then forces them to let go of their illusions, as well as some real possibilities. Since they are all characterized by great obstinance—and in this they thoroughly resemble Sisyphus—one can expect that new opportunities will emerge from the crisis unless they have so much energy to burn that even while experiencing a crisis, they just push the stone into the same old position. Here too they resemble Sisyphus: he was in the Underworld, but he returned unchanged into the upper world.

However, transformation is possible only when we are able to let go, when we can accept losses,[24] and ultimately, when we can accept the fact that gains and losses are a part of life. To return to a theme of the myth mentioned earlier, we have to accept that we must be not only "master thieves" but also "master losers." Being able to let go requires more courage than wanting to hold on. After all, we don't know how things will change when we let go. The myth only tells us what happens when we hold on longer than we should. But letting go can lead to the possibility of transformation.

An Example:
Letting Go Makes One Free

A couple, both around forty-five, were having enormous problems with one another. These difficulties emerged around the time when the children were leaving home, since the couple were now more focused on one another as a couple again. Both insisted that a separation or a divorce was out of the question. They tried to improve their relationship, went out together, did things, and finally ended up in couple's therapy. After a time it became clear that both were trying very hard to find a common basis, to develop common interests, and at the very least to express goodwill to one another. On the other hand, they both found each other restrictive, and would react allergically to each other's slightest idiosyncracies, whether of a verbal or physical nature. When the woman complained that her husband cleared his throat in such an awful way, I pointed out that he probably couldn't do anything about it, and that quite the contrary, it would most likely get worse as he got older. This very concrete example of mine was an injunction for the wife to accept her partner as he was at that moment, not as he could be once he had fulfilled all of her demands. This resulted in her suddenly talking about a possible separation.

The rule that stated they must stick together was put into question. Both of them renounced the security of the relationship and sacrificed the claim that it had to last forever. Doing so brought up a lot of fear. Both of them wondered what people would say and how they would get along by themselves, among other things.

Once they had both accepted the decision to face separation head on, they both took more liberties and started relating to each other in a completely new way. Suddenly they could share feelings with each other that they never before had shared.

Naturally one could see this development simply as a consequence of the fear of separation and being alone, fears which had arisen in both of them once they had given up the immutable safeguard that said they had to stay together. However, this new development also could mean that the possibility of having to let go opened up a potential way of staying together. Of course the two of them still had problems with each other, but they no longer functioned under the basic premise that nothing could be allowed to change in their relationship. This awareness brought with it the fact that problems could be tackled in a far more relaxed fashion.

This example shows that in real life neither holding on nor letting go is simple, but that the two are linked. Letting go of something that we are not already holding on to is not really letting go. The theme of the Sisyphus myth is, of course, more concerned with letting go since we have so much trouble doing that: we don't want to do it. As a whole, the myth also offers a countermand against letting go too easily, against giving up. From the beginning I have tried to view the pushing of the stone in light of this double aspect: the aspect of struggling in vain, and the aspect of irrepressible activity, stubbornness, courageous reapplication to the task, and concentration, to name just a few of the attributes.

Holding On and Letting Go

The courage that so impressed Camus—the courage to be obstinant and apply oneself even when no success is in view—is also imparted when we confront the myth. After all, we don't just hang on, we often let go much too soon. We are resigned, suffer from a sense of futility, and look at things that we have only just started as hopeless. Such an outlook can of course have many different causes, not all of which can be dealt with here. It is an outlook that accords death more space than life, stresses loss more than gain, and values destruction more than creativity. It is an outlook that gives all life the kiss of death just because we are all going to die. The human will, the power of resolve, and the ego are not believed capable of anything, while evil fate is deemed capable of everything. Ultimately this is the attitude that French existentialism turned against. In the face of the war, i.e., in the face of situations in which people seemed helpless, existentialism demanded that we reject this helplessness for as long as possible and do everything that lies within our power, even if the situation seems hopeless.

This attitude is illustrated in exemplary fashion in Camus's novel *The Plague*: A plague breaks out in the North African city of Oran, and an inexorable struggle arises between the inhabitants and the unstoppable spread of the epidemic, changing every aspect of life in the city, which must be closed off from the outside world. For Rieux, the local doctor, it is self-evident that he should fight against the sickness for as long as he is able, even if the same events keep occuring and he has no success in changing things:

> He folded back the bedsheet and shirt and silently regarded the red spots on the stomach and thighs and the swollen lymph glands. The mother looked at her daughter's inner thighs and cried out, without being able to control herself. Every evening mothers cried, their faces blank, over bodies that bore all the signs of death. Every evening people grasped at Rieux' arms, useless words tumbled out, promises, crying. Every evening the bells of the ambulance rang out uselessly, just like everyone's pain. And after this long sequence of similar evenings, Rieux could not hope for anything other than a long chain of similar events that would repeat themselves unendingly often. Indeed, the plague was as monotonous as an abstraction. There was perhaps only one thing that changed: Rieux himself. He realized this one evening at the foot of the statue of the republic. He was conscious only of a hard-won indifference that began to take hold of him, as he stared fixedly at the hotel enterance into which Rambert had disappeared.[25]

Rieux fights against death even though he knows that he will fail. With the same mind-set as Sisyphus, he tries to wrest from death its sacrifices, and to preserve as many people as possible before the separation:

> "At last. . . ," began the doctor, and again he hesitated, looking at Tarrou closely, "It is something that a man like you can understand, right? The order of the world is

determined by death, so perhaps it's better for God if we don't believe in him. We've got to fight with all our might against death, without turning our eyes to heaven where he is silent."

"Yes," agreed Tarrou, "I understand. But your victories will always be temporary, that's the only thing." Rieux's face seemed to darken.

"Always, I know. But that's no reason to give up the fight."

"No, it's not a reason. But now I can imagine what the plague must mean for you."

"Yes," said Rieux, "an endless defeat."[26]

Quite an opposite response comes from Rambert, a journalist who was in Oran quite by chance when the plague broke out. He has a wife whom he loves in Paris, and whom he longs for. He tries over and over again to get out of the closed city. He chooses to flee—and thus chooses love. When finally the possibility for escape seems likely, the people who are supposed to help Rambert are sick with the plague. Indignant, he says that he will have to start all over again, and suddenly he says: "You haven't yet understood that it [the plague] is all about starting over from the beginning."[27]

Having made this statement, Rambert decides to help Rieux in his voluntary medical service until he is able to leave the city. He, who had chosen love, now chooses charity. His beloved wife comes to the city when the plague is over. This struggle against the plague in the novel is impressive, even when the struggle seems thoroughly hopeless. The more hopeless the situation seems, the more people continue to fight, their courage growing in the hope that they will be able to bring the epidemic to a standstill.

But what does the plague symbolize? In the novel itself, Camus has an old asthmatic who is not himself sick with the plague, say, "But what does that mean, the plague? It's life, that's all."

Very often letting go quickly has something to do with an exalted goal, a goal that is nonetheless supposed to be attained very quickly. To be sure, Sisyphus is an example of an excessive person, but the anti-Sisyphus is, of course, also excessive. The goal is so exalted that it cannot possibly be attained; because of this, no energy can be freed to fulfill the goal. There are frequently people who are fixated in the extreme on some particular goal, yet the road or even the detours leading there, and the repeated effort required fill them with horror. In the face of this unsatisfying situation, such people are easily disheartened and give everything up for lost—and by doing so, they also give up themselves.

Letting go, giving up, making some authority, society, fate, or god completely responsible for everything that happens is an impulse against which we always must fight.

Sisyphus, on the other hand, is an example of someone who foregrounds his own power and will, who persists in the autonomy of his own ego.[28] He takes everything upon himself, only to keep on proving this autonomy. Even when the myth finally pronounces his struggle not humanly possible, he still embodies the very antithesis of this letting go of things, of surrendering to the life impulse of transience, of refusing to want to shape life creatively—even if we don't ultimately know to what extent that is possible.

The existential theme that is addressed in the myth of Sisyphus is the theme of autonomy and dependence, of expansion and moderation, of persevering according to one's own will and accepting one's limits. Ultimately, it has to do with the necessity of living life as intensely as possible, doing so in the face of death which is ever-present in the form of change, and of accepting these changes.

On this point the myth deals with only one aspect of life, namely active behavior. Sisyphus does after all work with his hands and feet; and besides being a voiceless hero, he is also a hero without love. Yet it is above all love that enables us to experience more life in the face of death. So it is not surprising that when people speak about Sisyphus, they talk overwhelmingly about a Sisyphean task. But actually this is something that needs to be looked at if we now consider the whole chain of associations: Is it a task that we burden ourselves with because we cannot let go, an idea that we cannot give up, or is it a task that may well be very difficult, but that is ultimately worthwhile, and worthwhile just for the sake of the experience, even if we don't attain our original goal?

This work needs to be thought of not only in the sense of something external that has to be overcome, but also as a task in and of itself. It is a conflict with a fundamental problem that we have to deal with. And it is this very conflict with a fundamental problem, irrespective of how similar it may seem each time, that brings us increasing autonomy during the course of our lives. However, as long as we are firmly convinced that such a problem has to be dealt with once and for all, then we will have to bear the stone with the uttermost reluctance whenever we are required to shoulder it again. If we can just accept that our basic problems only reveal themselves a bit at a time, and can only be worked on to a limited extent, then we will be able to shoulder the stone when we have to. This time we will see just how far we can get with it. Dealing with our "stones" becomes something else. We accept that everything keeps on repeating itself. It is the same, and yet each time it is also something new, the same stone, the same effort, and yet somehow we go the distance in a slightly different way. We learn different things along the way providing we are open to them and know that the distance that we have covered is the real goal. It is all about giving oneself over to the pulse of life, to the coming and going, the eternal return, and the conflict between life and death. Images associated with this might be the motion of the waves in the sea and the rising and setting of the sun. Whether we experience this eternal repetition as "over and over again" or as "ever new again" really depends upon whether we can accept this repetition, this return. We also have to accept that the repetition is also a "double take," that it takes something that would otherwise be lost. In other words, in this process of repetition and return something also comes back to us, something that we might easily lose to this state of transience. Finally, it has to do with whether we can accept a fundamental law that we always experience viscerally, or whether we believe that we have to put this fundamental law out of commission.

An Example: The Same Old Problem That Does Actually Change

A thirty-eight-year-old man says that all his life he has suffered from an inferiority complex. He comes from a family who made him feel excluded and inferior; aside from this he was a fragile child, something his family regarded as yet another sign of "inferiority." This theme of inferiority was then also the reason he sought therapy. According to him, he has tried during his entire life to set aside this feeling of inferiority; he made incredible demands of himself but still felt inferior, even though he knows that he is superior to most people in almost every regard, and naturally demands different things of himself than others. This "inferiority complex" coupled with considerable feelings of superiority is something akin to Sisyphus's stone that he must endlessly shoulder.

The therapeutic work that I am starting with him involves our trying to further develop aspects of his life that are still undeveloped, so that ultimately this fundamental problem can be outgrown, in keeping with Jung's basic assertion: "I had in the meantime learned to see that the greatest and most important life problems are all basically insoluble; . . . They can never be solved, only outgrown."[29] Naturally, we cannot avoid the fact that we have to deal with the basic problems that plague our everyday lives.

In the case of this man, this dilemma revealed itself in ever new forms. In the early stages of therapy, it was manifest in his being antagonistic to everyone. Then he was unhappy when people thought he was "unpleasant" and someone to be avoided. At a later stage, this rivalry retreated into the background somewhat. Instead he criticized other people's achievements to such an extent that in time he felt he was living in a world completely without value. Every poet, every composer, every painter, every scientist, every one of his contemporaries had absolutely nothing worth saying. Once he became aware of the fact that he was seeing his own root feeling—his fear that he had nothing worth saying—reflected in other people, he banished this outlook. Yet still he kept lapsing into these feelings. To be sure, in the meantime he had gotten to the point where he no longer demanded of himself that he be the wisest and cleverest of all. And in certain areas of his life he was thoroughly aware of his own self-worth. But then he suddenly started comparing himself to others again, being self-critical and envious during this next phase. Over and over again he tried to confront the feelings which came up in our therapy sessions. But once it became clear to him that this problem would accompany him for the rest of his life, it bothered him less when it resurfaced in such disruptive ways, threatening relationships. He started to see with great interest how the problem would manifest itself anew. It was no longer a matter of "yet again," but rather, "This time I felt a completely different kind of envy than in my last envy-attack. This time I wasn't just envious, I was also full of admiration for this colleague, and it was a warm admiration."

In reflecting and tracing how his problems with self-worth manifest themselves anew, in seeing how the stone he had to push looked again, and finding a course to set, he recalled all the journeys he had already taken with this problem and how much ground he had covered thanks to this problem. It was not simply a repetition, a reitteration of the same—it was this too—but within this repetition he also covered some new ground.

Repetition as an Aspect of the Creative Act

Resuming one's efforts is very clear in the example mentioned earlier of the painter who was unable to paint the image that she saw in her mind's eye, and who kept trying over and over again to accomplish the effect. Looking at her series of paintings, we see them as repetition—and yet it is clearly discernable that the form is always a little altered in favor of greater simplicity, something for which this painter was probably aiming.

In this case, the element of repetition affords the possibility of gradually approaching something that is not immediately expressible. And this seems to me quite typical of the creative process. Every creative person is seized by ideas that at some point or another have interested them before. During the course of life, they try to express what they really mean or whatever it is that is seeking expression through them. For many creative people, it is then the sum of what they have expressed that they really have to share. The journeys they have undertaken, and the traces of these journeys are what constitute the work, rather than some goal that they have attained.

The myth of Sisyphus is also a myth that portrays fundamental aspects of the creative process, if we assume that, as in the case of the painter, there is an inner image, an idea, a question that surfaces and needs to be continually worked through. The creative person can succeed in outwitting death to the extent that centuries after his or her death, the ideas and pictures still have an impact on people.

Above all, this myth deals with eternal repetition, something that also plays a part in creative endeavors. Such creativity is more a question of consistently sticking to some task rather than emulating the gods, though that intoxication may be associated with it as well. Sisyphus is after all no Prometheus.

It is the laborious aspect of creative endeavors that is depicted here. And here, too, the question arises as to when one should give up. The aforementioned painter worked stolidly and obsessively, as she herself put it, until one day she saw another picture that was more important to paint. She simply left the "old" sequence of pictures as they were—and years later effortlessly painted the picture that had actually floated before her. Having rolled the same stone for so long, she simply left it lying were it was, and shouldered it again some time later. For her there was no question as to when to shoulder the stone, and when to let go and leave the stone. These questions that are transmitted to our everyday lives via the myth were not a problem for her : she was open to ideas, and when one idea began to speak to her more strongly, then this is what she pursued. This openness is significant; it provides the possibility of circumventing the compulsion to repeat. Aside from this, what becomes very clear is that an inalienable part of the creative process is that we continually strive, come into conflict with the object of our creative work, and try to create consciously, but that this alone does not constitute the creative. To this must be added the idea that will not let itself be "realized." The idea however, having gone through many permutations, and a supposed return of the same, often arrives at its most effective form of expression. This process is perhaps what atists describe as wrestling with their genius. This notion could also be expressed in the myth of Sisyphus if we see the god Hermes or Apollo symbolically represented in the stone. But even then the stone would have to change over time and set an imperceptible new course.

Goethe formulates some thoughts on this issue:

1824, Tuesday, the 27th of January, 1824

People have always thought I was particularly blessed by good fortune. Nor do I want to complain and chide the course of my life. Basically it's been nothing but effort and work, and I might well say that in my seventy-five years there have not been four whole weeks of real comfort. It was the continual rolling of the stone that always had to be shouldered anew. My annals will make it clear what is meant by this. The demands made on my activities, both external and internal, were too many.[30]

As in the case of Goethe, it is clear that the "rolling of the stone" is a question of demands, both internal and external.

Once Again: Letting Go

In connection with the eternal repetition of the same task, it occured to me that people speak of "a labor of Sisyphus" not when the work itself is a great trial that can't be brought to an end, but rather when the eternal repetition and absence of change become torturous. This is how people talk when they love beginnings and new starts. In their own way they are unable to accept death, which after all brings an end, thereby establishing so much in our lives as part of a cycle of beginnings and ends, new beginnings and conclusions. They, too, do not let go enough, though they are impressive because they seem to be constantly letting go, since they only want the beginning and not the continuation. However, they do not let go of the idea that life should be the way they want it to be. They want perpetual spring. And because they cannot sacrifice this idea, they are unable to accept repetition. They are also not willing to see within the repetition what is new, nor can they comprehend the eternal repetition as the rhythm of human life, which can give structure to being, if we just consider for example, the fact that we periodically feel hungry.

When this repetition is combined with the weight of the stone that a person has to shoulder or thinks he must shoulder, then the question of letting go arises. Again there is the question of whether Sisyphus's efforts aren't perhaps being lived up to too heroically, and whether perhaps too little space and time are being left over for other aspects of life, issues which have been dealt with in other myths. Nonetheless, even Sisyphus could at least take a breather every now and again, namely when the stone went its own way, rolling of its own accord down into the valley. If one only sees the myth from the perspective of failure, then the stone slipping away from Sisyphus has to be seen as a "relapse." However, this could also represent the moment in which having given everything, we no longer have the stone in our control, when it goes its own way and we no longer have any influence. It would be pretty nonsensical to also want to control the stone as it rolled off down the hill. Yet this is just what many of us try to do.

An Example: Redemption

Some parents looked after their son for a long time, over and again they protected him, led him, and tried to guide him into a position that seemed right for him in life. They thought this wise, but also found it strenuous work. By the age of twenty-eight, the son had had enough of this very loving care. He said that he felt constantly pushed and pressured by his parents. He moved to another city. Both parents were very concerned about the fact that they no longer got any news about how his life was going. They spent all of their energy thinking of ways in which they could still control their son without frustrating him. They thought this was their job, and would have felt bad had they given any less thought to this problem.

Obviously the parents could not let go, particularly because they had concentrated on their son to such an extent that his life had become the central focus of their lives. They could not let go even when he had already slipped away from them.

At least Sisyphus did not still attempt to control the stone when it was rolling away. We do not actually know how he dealt with the descent into the valley, whether he enjoyed the passing freedom, or whether he was beset by thoughts of having to shoulder the stone again as soon as possible. But this would be, as with all Sisyphean tasks, the moment of exhaling, the moment of breathing deeply. Now Sisyphus would be able to let his shoulders drop, and to turn his gaze away from the stone that he has to push and look around at his surroundings. Even if the stone has to be shouldered over and over again, there is always the rhythm between breathing out and lifting. But we can relinquish this rhythm if we don't let the departing stone out of our sight and always think about it too much.

The Myth of
the Forty-Year-Old

If we assume that the central message of this myth is that on the one hand we must accept death and on the other hand we must outwit it—in the sense of not surrendering too easily to life's transience—then it is no wonder that the people who are the ones most affected by this myth are those at about the age of forty.

By mid-life, it is no longer possible to deny the fact that we are going to die, that life is heading for death. Moreover, this is a phase in which many things that have worked well up until now must be dispensed with. The high-flown plans of youth which gave life some direction, appeal, and challenge are all spent. The collision of the impossible with the possible has shown what our limitations are—not rigid limitations, but flexible ones, though not limitations that can be pushed to eternity. We learn that we may well be ordinary people, but also that we have to be ordinary people. Being able to be ordinary and having to be ordinary means that we say goodbye to many of the big ideas and exaggerated claims that we once had.

Associated with this is, on the one hand, a perpetual good-bye, on the other, an increasing degree of freedom. Saying good-bye also means freedom—from ideas, values, demands upon us and others. Being ordinary opens up lots of ordinary life options.

The recognition that lots of things in life repeat themselves occurs more and more frequently and unavoidably. Often we tell ourselves that we know "that"—which has to do not only with the many repetitions in everyday life, but also with repetitions of nice (or painful) experiences about ourselves. But repetitions are also apparent in the next generation: longings, hopes, demands, protests recur, as does the way of dealing with the problems. As we all know, even fashion and the taste associated with it recur.

If we worry only about the fact that so very much in life repeats itself, and do not access the respective situations within the repetitions, we will soon find ourselves looking for something impossible.

During this phase, the problem of aging, of growing older, consists mainly of the fact that these repetitions have to be accepted as structural elements of passing time and thus of death, which is creeping up on us. We also have to accept that we cannot just exhaust our capacity for experience by simply accepting repetition and lamenting it. It may be the same old stone, but we are capable of going different routes with it. The great breakthrough that we once hoped for, takes place if at all, in small steps and comes out of these repetitions which suddenly provide new experiences.

Aside from this, it becomes increasingly clear that we have to take our own life into our hands if anything at all is going to happen. We can no longer ascribe the blame to other people. The society that we criticize is also the society we ourselves constitute—as is evident from the fact that people of this age are often in positions in which they must make decisions. They have had enough experience to enable such decision-making, and they also have enough energy to carry out these decisions and the work associated with them. Feelings of self-worth are no longer nourished by the big ideas that they were going to put into effect sometime or other, but rather from what they actually achieve, from what is tangible and visible.

The conscious awareness that death is everpresent makes life valuable, and allows us to look for the vivacity in life. This places the theme of Sisyphus into a wider context: in a positive sense, it means that we try not to let anything in life be in vain, that we keep concentrating on whatever it is that needs to be done, and that we devote ourselves to the task that we have set for ourselves. We accept that the effort accomplishes something, but that it may not be able to move mountains. Youth, which of course still lurks in every forty-year-old, continues to want to storm the mountain top. For each of us at this age, accepting human limitations means accepting eternal repetition, including boredom and unproductiveness. And if these all-too-youthful qualities—the Hermes-like aspects of Sisyphus —cannot be relinquished, then the predominating feeling in life is one of pointlessness: everything becomes absurd and meaningless.

But these feelings also come alive when one applies Sisyphus exclusively to the work world—and the question then becomes what is the point of leading such a life. It might well be time to let go of the stone, to give up the experience of heroic struggle that one goes through every day, and to experience other things. At the same time, one might consider whether it isn't perhaps time to let go all together. After all, though Sisyphus can't actually implement his grandiose plan to get the stone over the top of the mountain, his struggle is still splendidly heroic. And this heroism is what we human beings use as a way of creating value that will hopefully outlast us. Yet persistently fulfilling our duties can also be seen as a way of combatting death and impermanence. In so doing, we try to suppress the fact that we are mortal. This is particularly clear when we are not prepared to let go, when we have to prove over and over again that we are capable of doing something. When this is the case, then we are precluded from experiencing other areas of life, mostly because in our society being busy, active, and productive are qualities that are very highly valued.

Other Interpretations of the Sisyphus Myth

Sisyphus as Healer

In his dictionary of Greek and Roman myths, W. H. Rosher[31] offers various different interpretations of the myth. He states for example, that tying up Death also expresses the fact that Sisyphus had found a healing substance; his return from the realm of the dead would thus be seen as representing a recovery from a severe illness. This interpretation is thoroughly comprehensible and goes along with my expanded interpretation. It does however omit the punishment. Were Sisyphus a real healer, however, then he would have wanted to overcome death at any price. If it were ever possible to completely free people from death, then the most logical consequence would be for him to carry his burden forever, since he would not be able to die.

Rolling the Stone: The Work of the Waves

Sisyphus is linked predominantly to the sea, first of all as "an allegory of the helpless, rolling, all-penetrating

sea" or he is compared with "a tide: its restless,
changeable, rolling, perpetually active, nature that
penetrates to the deepest depths and surfaces again."
"His punishment in the Underworld is probably
nothing other than a poetic look at the untiring work
of the waves of the sea which wash from east and west
against the rocks of the isthmus without being able to
reach high ground."[32]

Until this point we have transplanted ourselves into the image
of the stone-rolling Sisyphus and experienced the whole ordeal
along with him. Now this image is replaced with that of the
waves of the sea. What was previously superhuman, heroic exertion, suddenly becomes a part of a perfectly natural rhythm. It
becomes an expression of the energy lurking in the sea, the
rhythm of all that is living.

Notions of repetition, return, and rhythm are supported by
the suggestions posed by this interpretation. However, in surrendering exertion to the sea, we lose our sense of identification
with the hero Sisyphus, whether we feel an affinity with him, or
whether we reject this kind of heroism.

Sisyphus Rolling the Sun

One scholar quoted by Rosher[33] sees a hero of light in Sisyphus; in the stone that he rolls, the sun; and in the ascent and
descent, the rising and setting of the sun. Yet, such an interpretation would imply that the stone disappears down the other
side of the hill, something that is not substantiated elsewhere.
Robert Graves also speaks of the stone of Sisyphus as being the
stone of someone who rolls the sun, referring to a well-docu-
mented Corinthian cult of the sun and seeing Sisyphus as
Helios, the god of the sun and of light.[34]

From my point of view, the stone itself symbolically could
be linked to Hermes or perhaps Apollo. The idea here that the

sun is pushed across the sky cannot be denied out of hand, even if the motion of the sun doesn't correspond to the motion of the stone. Consistent with this is the theme of rising and setting, the theme of rhythm entailed in climbing and falling. If we regard the sun from a symbolic perspective, then the heroic efforts of mankind could represent the attempt to introduce more and more light into the world, to become ever more aware. This too requires an effort. It always brings a certain degree of progress, yet we also keep regressing.

Striving for Awareness

This interpretation would be similar to the another one posed in the Roscher book:

> The rolling of the stone of Sisyphus can be understood as the futile striving for human reason. Just when he thinks he is on the point of attaining his goal and swinging over the last obstacle at the top, he falls back, exhausted from the useless exertion.[35]

This interpretation depicts the human being as someone who always wants to overcome the final hurdle, as Ingeborg Bachmann describes in her story, "The Thirtieth Year":

> Once, when he was barely twenty years old, he had thought everything to its end in the Vienna national library and then found that he was alive after all. He lay over the books like a drunkard and thought about things while the little green lamps burned and the readers crept by on cat feet, quietly coughed, quietly turned pages, as though they were afraid of waking the ghosts that lived between the letters on the page. He thought—if someone understands what that means! He still knows exactly the moment he traced a logic problem, when all the concepts lay loose and maneuverable in his head. And then he thought and thought and flew higher and higher as though on a swing, without feeling dizzy, and then he gave himself

the best thrust of all: he felt himself fly into a ceiling through which he had to go. Feelings of joy like never before had come over him because in this moment he was on the threshold of understanding something that encompassed it all. He would push through with his next thought! Then it happened. A blow struck him, somewhere inside his head: There was pain which forced him to leave off, he slowed his thoughts, became confused, and leaped from the swing. He had transgressed his capacity for thinking, or perhaps it was just that no human being can think beyond the place he had attained. Up there, in his head, in his skull, something clicked, it clicked frighteningly and wouldn't stop even for a moment. He thought he had gone crazy and scrunched up his book with his hands. He let his head flop forward and closed his eyes, unconscious in full consciousness.

He was finished."[36]

A human experience to be sure, but people such as this glean from Sisyphus only one part of the story, the part about storming the top. In the context of this story, this means wanting to know more and more, something that can also be associated with carrying the sun. People like this don't have the perseverance, the tenacity with which Sisyphus keeps on pushing his stone.

The Myth As an Expression of the Character of People Who Live by the Sea

Sisyphus is also seen as a representative of the "crafty coastal dwellers in contradistinction to the simplicity of inland dwellers."[37] This source, meanwhile, speaks of a merchant who never rests and is always on the go. And Roscher writes:

> The conclusion to be drawn from these various interpretations of the Sisyphus myth is as follows: The activity of the sea—a natural drama of eternal return, particularly evident on the shores of Corinth—is united in the figure of a person.

The effects of a life on the sea are then embodied in this person. A single characteristic that they bear is regarded as a punishment, and a motive is sought for this punishment. A later allegorical-ethical influence on the form of the story is accepted by some and rejected by others.[38]

This interpretation, of which there are many similar ones, I find particularly interesting because it shows that everyone who deals with the myth emphasizes particular characteristics and that they represent whatever has been evoked in them by the myth in the form of thoughts and images. I mean that all myth interpretation—and so too this one—occurs in this fashion, even if some individual characteristics are stressed more than others and some not at all. Dealing with a myth also means, apart from other things, that the myth conjures up associations which establish links with our own lives. As such, we don't interpret the myth so much as our existential experience in the mirror of the myth.

The Myth of Sisyphus
in Dreams

A Summary

That myths are images that have an impact on everyday life and remain meaningful to us today is revealed not only in our language, which uses expressions like "a labor of Sisyphus," but also in our dreams, which adopt these images and interweave them with personal images from the lives of individuals.

The Dream of a Thirty-Eight-Year-Old Woman:
One Can't Snatch Anything away from Death

"I was on a very steep mountain. Small cars that look like coal trucks were rolling down the mountain. Inside the cars were people who looked as though they were a step away from death. I was upset about how lethargic they were, how they were just letting everything happen to them. I wanted to get someone out of there. And I did manage to grab someone. I carried the person almost from the valley floor to the top of the mountain—it was a really high one. I was sweating like crazy, but I carried this person up the whole mountain; it was really hard. I've never had a such a sweaty dream. The sweat was running down me in streams. I don't know whether the person I schlepped was a man or a woman; the person was also naked, a living corpse, already half-dead. I had the feeling that if I could bring this person to the top of the mountain, then he or she would make it over the top. Up there, there was life. I tried three times and twice the person rolled back down. The third time, when I was almost at the top—there were just two or three meters to go— I already had the feeling that I had finally done it. It was a feeling of triumph and joy. But suddenly a huge black figure loomed up before me like a wall and just threw me back into the valley. I stumbled back. I resisted and woke up. And at this moment I knew: That was Death. The person slipped down from me and rolled into the valley again. I had the feeling of being completely and truly defeated."

The Dreamer's Interpretations

"I knew that I was resisting because my partner was awakened by my slamming back against the bed from a sitting position. My arm was sore, the same arm that I used to resist the figure in the dream. In the dream I had the feeling that I was being grabbed by a terrible force. Thrown back—no, it was more like being slammed back. It was an enormous figure that turned into a black wall. I just knew in the dream that it was Death and you can't take anything away from Death. The person then rolled back down into the valley.

"These people almost reminded me of a concentration camp, of people condemned to die. It really upset me that they didn't do anything. I ran behind the trucks and told them they had to do something, and then I tugged them out of the trucks. Still, two of them just rolled down into the valley, but the third

I carried with the sweat of my brow, and when I was almost at the top, suddenly this figure appeared and I fought. But Death really hammered me. Then I lay down on my back.

"The dream has something to do with my everyday life: I'd just been dealing with a suicidal patient whom I wanted to save at any cost. It was my psychiatry training period and I had the feeling that I could really do something, that I could motivate people. The way they were resigned to their fate really got me going: The sense of sacrifice that they exhibited, the way they just let themselves be carried off! I wanted to outwit Death somehow.

"During this time I was incredibly active. I was convinced that I could change fate for the better. Especially with this suicidal patient—she's still alive by the way—and then suddenly I had this dream that showed up my human limitations or how extreme my situation was. What became obvious was all my rebelliousness at that time, and with one blow my rebelliousness was given a limit.

"After this dream I changed a lot. I was better able to resign myself to fate. Before the dream I had this arrogant notion that one could get somewhere with these lost souls if only one could grab onto them; if one could overcome this inertia then one could snatch them away from Death. Today I am much more composed in these kind of situations. I accompany people. But when someone really wants to or has to go through the gateway of death, then I can accept it. Of course I always try to stop them from dying, but I don't use force anymore.

"Death was an enormous figure, sort of indeterminate. You could only see a cloak; he was covered up and incredibly powerful, impenetrable, and terrible. He doesn't at all correspond to my idea of a gentle death. But he didn't kill me, he just pushed me back. Then I was lying in the dirt and I also felt like dirt. Sort of in the sense, 'You worm, there you are.'

But the feeling of life in the dream before Death cast me aside, that was great: It was pretty arrogant. I was gloating inside, triumphant. There was also so much at stake in this schlepping, the feeling of totally giving myself over to the task, of being absorbed in the task, an experience of my own power.

"I thought of Camus in regard to this dream: For him this schlepping had almost an orgiastic quality to it. And this is what it was for me too."

This dream is thoroughly infused with the myth of Sisyphus. In the end, the dreamer thinks of Camus, and Camus is frequently associated with the work of Sisyphus. When I heard about my colleague's dream, which she has so kindly let me use in this book, I was totally spellbound. I was impressed by the rebelliousness and incredible task that the dreamer took upon herself. But I was just as paralyzed by the figure of Death who so clearly set limits. Although she dreamed this dream five years ago, she told it to me as though it had just happened.

Resisting Death, and so clearly being put in check by him, seems to me to be the core of the dream—and for me this is also the main tenet of the myth of Sisyphus. This is also evident from the way the dreamer describes this part of the dream. She goes into it in great detail and keeps on coming back to it, a sign of how important this part and this experience is for her.

Attempt at an Interpretation

The dreamer finds herself on a very high mountain. Getting to the top would take a great effort, but also be associated with a big demand. She herself says in the dream that she has the feeling that if she could get these half-dead people up the mountain, then they would be as good as over the top. At the top there is life. "Being over the hump" is the expression used to signify that someone has gotten over a sickness or a difficulty; they have conquered a mountain of difficulties. In the context of the dream text, overcoming difficulties would also mean life, being able to enter the land of the living.

The coal trucks however aren't moving up the hill, they are going down. Nor is there any coal in the coal trucks. There are people who "look as though they are at death's door," who submit to everything. These people seem to be going "down hill"— comparable to the stone rolling down the mountain in the myth of Sisyphus—they can't stop it, they let it happen to them, they have "let go." This attitude rattles the dreamer to the core. She speaks of lethargy, of inertia, of being resigned to fate, but also of the fact that these people remind her of concentration camps, of people condemned to die. If they have been condemned to die then some power has condemned them and the dreamer appears as a dream-ego to confront this power. She cannot bear this inertia, this letting go.

The opposites of letting go and holding on are depicted in the images of the half-dead people and the dream-ego. The people in the coal trucks only let go; the dream-ego, which counteracts passivity, only holds on wanting to reach the summit. As such, one can't really speak of "letting go" when it comes to the people in the coal trucks. It is more a case of "surrendering," of "giving up."

Having to let go and holding on at any price was a subject that concerned us in our treatment of the myth. In this context, by schlepping people up the mountain, the dream-ego really identifies with Sisyphus, although remaining convinced that success is actually possible. There is no discernable hopelessness in the dream-ego. On the contrary, the dream-ego confronts resignation with a great deal of hope. The strenuous task is described impressively: the sweat-attacks, the feeling of being engaged in the task, the total devotion to it, the feeling of power. And in recalling Camus's treatment of Sisyphus, the almost "orgiastic" aspect of the situation is emphasized. It is not only exhausting work; there are moments of an intense feeling of being at one with the self, an incredible experience of self.

That these people rolled down the mountain twice is something that the dreamer mentions only in passing. It was schlepping them up the hill that was important, not the disappointment. Schlepping them up the mountain was so important that the dream-ego would have put up with even more failure on their account. The dreamer does not notice the gender of these people who are already almost dead. They are simply people who have to be on the mountain in order to make it over the top. It has nothing to do with personal relationships, it has to do with performing a service on behalf of mankind. Over and over again it is emphasized that these people are already all but dead, and it becomes increasingly clear that the dream-ego wants to snatch them away from Death. Here is where the first part of the myth comes into play: With all its might, the dream-ego wants to deny death something that is already his preserve. On the third attempt, the dream-ego almost makes it—the dream-ego is right at the top, already happy and triumphant. And when you hear this dream you feel the need to breathe a sigh of relief along with the dream-ego. But then suddenly a huge black figure rises up before her and throws her back into the valley. This event is variously described: as the feeling of being seized by an incredible force that counteracts everything she has, which she ultimately cannot oppose. She feels not only cast back, but slammed back. Surrendering, she lies on her back. In the dream, Death is depicted as he so often is as concealed, impenetrable, terrible. The dreamer mentions that he does not correspond to her idea of a gentle death. To me this would seem to make sense. After all, he isn't coming to her as death in the final sense; he is death for this arrogant ego, for this ego which wants to turn itself into a god. In other words, death introduces the necessity for a fundamental transformation of her attitude. This woman cannot spend her whole life ecstatically, orgiastically schlepping half-dead people up mountain sides. Death proves that he is stronger than she is. The death of this arrogant side occurs, making this struggle with Death, almost a fight to the death. The dreamer then feels vulnerable. She uses the words "dirt" and "worm," the very opposite of hubris, of the divine, of this triumphant feeling that human beings can distinguish themselves. The black wall that is associated with death in this dream clearly shows that the dreamer cannot go any further. She has to let go of the hubris. She has not been killed; only one aspect of her has been killed.

The intensity of this struggle is revealed by the fact that she sat up in bed, she fought physically, as though it really were a matter of life and death. And it became clear to her: in the final analysis, we can't take anything away from Death. The person she carried up the mountain rolls down into the valley again.

In the myth of Sisyphus, there is no Death on the mountain. Yet still we get the impression that it is the principle of death that does not allow the stone to be rolled over the mountain.

The dreamer links this dream to a suicidal patient and the beginning of her psychiatric work. This dream expresses her tremendous involvement with people, her skill and resolve, but also the hubris of the caregiver and healer's personality that fights against death, against lethargy and surrendering to fate.

From her actions the "rebelliousness of that time" also becomes clear. She is rebelling, as she puts it, against the fact that people suffer so much. So seen, the doctor who carries those half-dead people almost becomes the one to right this wrong. However, the hubris that we have already seen in the case of

Sisyphus always distinguishes those people who are seized by the desire to help and who know neither their limitations nor their measure. This measure is what is determined by Death.

If we follow the vein of interpretation offered by the dreamer, then the question arises as to whether human life should be saved at any cost. Should people be saved even when they are set on another course (as in the dream)—namely on their way into the valley—when they later might be able to climb up the mountain themselves? The dreamer then says that she has learned from the dream. She has learned to accompany suicidal people, to lead them away from the edge, but no longer to do so with force. She is also able to accept their resolve: something that is incredibly difficult, yet which is an absolute prerequisite if one is to be able to work with suicidal people at all.

The half-dead people which the dreamer obviously associates with people who have suicidal tendencies and no life force can also be seen as representing different aspects in the psyche of the dreamer. The people who are resigned to fate embody aspects of the dreamer which give up too easily—and this is something that the dream-ego cannot accept at all. Letting go, giving something up for lost, giving up does not seem to fit into the scheme of the dream-ego. In other words, this means that death does actually effect our lives and our psyches. This is something that the dream-ego wants to reverse, to make impossible. This not-wanting-to-live is situated in the concentration camp, that is to say, it is made the consequence of a very destructive force. It might well be that the dreamer sees this having to give up as the consequence only of a very destructive force and not as part of the natural rhythm of life. It is no wonder then that she fights against this force. Aside from this it is conceivable that embodied in these half-dead people are some suicidal tendencies on the part of the dreamer. They may even be suicidal for the very reason that she experiences the principle of letting go too little in her life. Death however makes it very clear: There is death, there is failure: it is all part of it.

Clearly expressed in this dream is the fact that we all are forced to let go. If we are not prepared to do so at the right moment, then whatever it is that we should have let go of is going to be wrenched away from us.

In considering the theme of holding on and letting go, it becomes clear that we do not exclusively hold on or let go. There are probably some aspects of life that we hold onto too tightly, others that we let go of too easily. Establishing a good rhythm between holding on and letting go is known as moderation. Yet knowing the right balance isn't something we are born with. It seems to me that we have to keep on being tested and then accept the fact that human beings have limitations. This balance is not something that is established once and for all; it is something we probably have to strive for during the course of a lifetime.

This is true not only for us as individuals, it is also true for mankind as a whole. Without presumptuousness there is no progress, and without modesty no responsibility—something that also makes this progress meaningful to human beings.

Notes

Ali Baba and the Forty Thieves

1. From *Märchen aus 1001 Nacht (Fairy Tales from 1001 Nights)*, narrated by Vladimir Hulpach, appearing in the series "Märchen der Welt (Fairy Tales of the World)" (Hanau, Germany: Werner Dausien Press, 1982). The original version which I occasionally refer to can be found in *Die Erzählungen aus den Tausendundein Nächten (Tales from a Thousand and One Nights)*, translated from the original Arabic text by Enno Littmann (Frankfurt, Germany: Insel Press, Frankfurt, 1928), vol. 4, 791–859.

2. Hulpach translation, 11–17. In the Insel Press version, Scheherban is described as Schehrijar (ruler), Schahseman as Schazaman (greatest king of his time). Dinarsad is presumably the servant rather than the sister of Scheherazade; vol. 12, 668.

3. Littmann, vol. 4, 645.

4. Ibid.

5. Cf. Verena Kast, *Märchen als Therapie (Fairy Tales as Therapy)*, (Olten: Walter Press, 1986).

6. Cf. Verena Kast, *Wege zur Autonomie* (Olten: Walter Press, 1985).

7. Cf. on this topic also Hans Dieckmann, *Individuation in den Märchen aus 1001 Nacht* (Fellbach-Öffingen: Bonz Press, 1974).

8. Cf. Verena Kast, "Zum Umgang der Märchen mit dem Bösen," "Der Dreißiger" and "Der Blaubart", in *Das Böse im Märchen* by M. Jacoby, V. Kast, and I. Riedel (Fellbach-Öffingen: Bonz Press, 1978).

9. Hulpach, 14.

10. These interpretations are drawn from the original [Littmann] text which could not be used on account of its length. The story of "Ali Baba and the Forty Thieves" is in vol. 4, 791–859.

11. Ibid., 791.

12. Annemarie Schimmel, *Mystische Dimensionen des Islam. Die Geschichte des Sufismus*, Cologne: Diederichs Press, 1985, 51 [English edition: *The Mystical Dimensions of Islam* (Chapel Hill: University of North Carolina Press, 1975)].

13. Ibid., 478.

14. "Der goldene Vogel," in *Kinder- und Hausmärchen, gesammelt durch die Brüder Grimm* (Frankfurt: Insel Press, 1979).

15. Schimmel, 143.

16. Ibid., 286.

17. Littmann, vol. 4, 796–97.

18. Ibid. 798.

19. Ibid. 795, footnote.

20. *Herder Lexikon griechische und römische Mythologie (Herder Dictionary of Greek and Roman Mythology)*. revised by Dorothea Coenen (Freiburg: Herder Press, 1986).

21. Erich Neumann, *Die große Mutter* (Olten: Walter Press, 1956/1974), 251. [English version: *The Great Mother: An Analysis of the Archetype* (Princeton: Princeton University Press, 1975).

22. Ibid, 57.

23. Schimmel, 413.

24. Littmann, vol. 4, 802.

25. Abbreviated from Verena Kast, *Sisyphus. Der alte Stein—der neue Weg*, Zurich: Kreuz Press, 1986, 59 ff.

26. Ingrid Riedel, ed. *Kreis, Kreuz, Dreieck, Quadrat, Spirale* (Stuttgart: Kreuz Press, 1985), 42.

27. Schimmel, 146.

28. Neumann, 272.

29. Littmann, vol. 4, 842.

30. Ibid.

31. Ibid., 847.

32. Neumann, 281.

The Myth of Sisyphus

1. Homer, *The Odyssy*, XI, 593 (From a German translation by A. Weiher).

2. Ibid.

3. Goethe, J. W. von, in *Goethes Werkes* (Hamburg, 1963), vol. 12, 516 [English translation: *The Maxims and Reflections of Goethe*, trans. Bailey Saunders (New York/London: Macmillan & Co., 1893)].

4. Albert Camus, *Le mythe de Sisyphe* (Paris: Librairie Gallimard, 1942), 100 [English translation: *The Myth of Sisyphus* (New York: Alfred A. Knopf, 1955)].

5. Ibid.

6. Cf. O.F. Bollnow, *Neue Geborgenheit—Das Problem einer Überwindung des Existentialismus* (Stuttgart, 1955), 94.

7. Cf. Marcel, "Entwurf einer Phänomenologie und einer Metaphysik der Hoffnung," in *Philosophie der Huffnung* (Munich, 1964).

8. Ingeborg Bachmann, *Werke*, ed. Christine Koschel, Inge von Weidenbaum, and Clemens Münster (Munich/Zurich: Piper, 1978), 253 [English translation: in the short story collection, *The Thirtieth Year*, trans. by Michael Bullock (New York: Alfred A. Knopf, 1964)].

9. Ibid, 254.

10. Ibid, 260.

11. *Herder Lexikon der Symbole*, (Freiburg: Herder, 1978), 161. [English edition: *The Herder Dictionary of Symbols* (Wilmette, Ill.: ChironPublications, 1986)].

12. Herbert Hunger, *Lexicon der griechischen und römischen Mythologie* (Reinbeck by Hamburg, 1974); see also Robert Graves, *The Greek Myths* (New York: George Braziller, 1955) [German edition, von Ranke–Graves, *Griechische Mythologie* (Hamburg, 1982)].

13. Cf. W. H. Roscher, ed., *Ausführliches Lexikon deer griechischen und römischen Mythologie* (Leipzig, 1909–15), 958 ff.

14. M. Grant and J. Hazel, eds., *Lexikon der antiken Mythen und Gestalten* (Munich, 1980).

15. Von Ranke–Graves, 194.

16. Cf. Hunger, 176ff.; and von Ranke–Graves, 52 ff.

17. Cf. Plato, *Phaedrus*, Paragraph 33c.

18. Cf. C. Helbling, ed., *Kinder- und Hausmarchen der Gebruder Grimm* (Zurich, n.d.), 192 .

19. Cf. Karl Kerenyi, *Die Mythologie der Griechen* (Munich, 1966), vol. 2 .

20. Cf. Franz Ré Soupault, *Marchen* (Düsseldorf/Cologne, 1963), 71 ff.

21. Williams, in Verena Kast, *Trauern—Phasen und Chancen des psychischen Prozesses* (Stuttgart: Kreuz, 1986), 158.

22. Cf. J. Bolte and G. Polivka, *Anmerkkungen zu den Kinger- und Hausmärchen der Brüder Grimm* (Olms: 1963), vol. 1, 378 f.

23. Helbling, 299.

24. Cf. Kast, *Trauern*.

25. Cf. Albert Camus, *La Peste* (Paris: Librairie Gallimard, 1947), 60 f. [English translation: *The Plague* (New York: Alfred A. Knopf, 1948).]

26. Ibid, 84 f.

27. Ibid, 107.

28. Cf. Kast, *Wege zur Autonomie* (Olten, 1985).

29. C. G. Jung, *Des Geheimnis der goldenen Blüte* (Zurich, 1929), 12 [English translation: *The Secret of the Golden Flower* (New York: Harcourt, Brace & World, 1962)].

30. Goethe, in Johann P. Eckermann, *Gepräche mit Goethe* (Leipzig, 1948) [English translation: *Speaking with Goethe* (Munchen: C. H. Beck, 1982)].

31. Cf. Roscher, 967 f.

32. Ibid, 967.

33. Cf. Henry (1892), in Roscher, 967.

34. Cf. von Ranke–Graves, 197.

35. Cf. Völker, in Roscher, 968.

36. Ingeborg Bachmann, *Das dreißigste Jahr* (Munich, 1961), 25 [English translation: *The Thirtieth Year* , trans. Michael Bullock (New York: Alfred A. Knopf, 1964)].

37. Cf. Curtius, in Roscher, 968.

38. Roscher, 969 f.